MOTHER, NATURE

MOTHER, NATURE

*A 5,000-Mile Journey to Discover if
a Mother and Son Can Survive
Their Differences*

. . .

JEDIDIAH JENKINS

CONVERGENT

NEW YORK

Published in the United States by Convergent Books,
an imprint of Random House, a division of
Penguin Random House LLC, New York.

CONVERGENT BOOKS is a registered trademark and the Convergent
colophon is a trademark of Penguin Random House LLC.

LIBRARY OF CONGRESS CATALOGING-IN-PUBLICATION DATA
Names: Jenkins, Jedidiah, author.
Title: Mother, nature / by Jedidiah Jenkins.
Description: New York, NY: Convergent Books, [2023]
Identifiers: LCCN 2023020999 (print) | LCCN 2023021000 (ebook) |
ISBN 9780593137260 (hardcover) | ISBN 9780593137277 (ebook)
Subjects: LCSH: Jenkins, Jedidiah—Travel—United States. | Jenkins,
Barbara—Travel—United States. | United States—Description and travel. |
Travel writers—United States—Biography. | Gay men—Family
relationships—United States. | Mother and son—United States.
Classification: LCC E169.Z83 J46 2023 (print) |
LCC E169.Z83 (ebook) | DDC 917.304—dc23/eng/20230602
LC record available at https://lccn.loc.gov/2023020999
LC ebook record available at https://lccn.loc.gov/2023021000
Ebook ISBN 978-0-593-13727-7

Illustrations by Jedidiah Jenkins

Printed in the United States of America on acid-free paper

convergentbooks.com

2 4 6 8 9 7 5 3 1

First Edition

Book design by Edwin A. Vazquez

*To little Jed
who thought it would all fall apart
and he would lose everything,
even his mom*

This rupture between parents and their children is what happens, over and over, with every new generation; there is nothing for it, no remedy, no answer. Who is right ... They're both right, and they're both wrong, and neither will ever understand the other.

—Keith Gessen,
reviewing Ivan Turgenev's
Fathers and Sons for
The New Yorker

The road has its own reasons and no two travelers will have the same understanding of those reasons. If indeed they come to an understanding of them at all.

—Cormac McCarthy,
The Crossing

MOTHER, NATURE

1

· · ·

Let me begin with a parable. It comes from India. "The Blind Monks and the Elephant." It goes like this:

There is a group of blind monks living on the edge of town. They have lived in their monastery for many years, passing the time in peace and prayer. Until one day, when a strange new animal is brought to the village. It is called an "elephant." Word of its arrival spreads to every house, and crowds form in the town square, day and night. The monks decide that they want to go experience this creature. They've never heard of such a thing, and they want to touch it. They hurry to the town square, where they hear the murmurs of a large crowd and a new sound, the grumble of an animal that must be very large. They make their way through the townspeople and now the monster's groans are very close.

The first monk walks up and touches the left tusk, amazed at its size. Another feels the trunk, running his hands along the powerful snaking appendage. Another gently traces his fingers around the giant flapping ear. Another its leg. There are many people surrounding the elephant, touching it where they can. Before long, the monks' time is up. There is a line, of course, and a short man in uniform sends them on their way.

The monks walk home stupefied, filled with the wonder of something bigger than their imagination. They are laughing and holding hands. They are electrified, talking fast and over each other. "What a wonder! A giant made entirely of bone!" "Bone? No, it was a leathery winged creature." "What are the two of you saying? It was a ten-foot-tall hairy snake!" To each monk's dismay, none of their stories align. "I know that it was bone, I touched it, and how can you say otherwise?" Something about the arguing makes the men double down on their memories, certain not only of their picture of the elephant, but that the others must be delusional. First they raise their voices, then they are shouting. "You're a liar!" "How dare you call me a liar!" And then fists are swinging.

In many versions of the story, the community of monks falls apart and they go their separate ways.

On January 1, 2003, I flipped my car. I was home from college, driving to my friend Adam's house on the morning of New Year's Day. You may guess that I was hungover. I was not. I was a good Christian boy who thought drinking was for losers. But I had stayed up late, drinking Martinelli's sparkling cider and playing Catch Phrase with my Christian friends.

When I left my mom's house, it was perhaps 10 A.M., and it had just begun to rain. I heard somewhere that the road is slickest just as the rain begins, because the water lifts the accumulated soot and dirt off the asphalt, making it slippery. I was driving my mom's extra car, a Ford Explorer from the early nineties. The seat belts didn't latch. The tires were bald, as smooth as marble. But I didn't think about any of that. I was young, and I got in the car with no seat belts and bald tires because I wanted to hang out with my friends and play Nintendo 64. The drive was only a few miles, but it snaked through the hills south of Nashville. S-curved rivers of pavement connecting neighborhoods hidden in maple, buckeye, and oak.

That morning, I was playing Tori Amos's "A Sorta Fairytale" loud and full in the doomed car. I remember being thrilled when she sang about driving "up on the 101," as I finally knew what that was, going to college in Los Angeles.

On Granny White Pike, while navigating a curve that is now forever burned into my limbic system, I felt my car detach from the normal rules of physics. My stomach knew before my mind. I was floating, disconnected from the road, and rotating. Adrenaline tingled across my rib cage. The car spun counterclockwise, turning perpendicular to the lane I'd been driving in, at which point the tires found just enough purchase to launch the vehicle off the road.

On both sides of the road were steep, upward sloping hills. My car jammed itself up the incline, crunching bushes like paper lanterns, and then barrel-rolled back down into the ditch. Remember, my seat belt didn't buckle, so as the vehicle began rolling, I was ripped from the driver's seat, my legs dragging across the gearshift like noodles. My head slammed into the passenger window, breaking it, then the car rolled again and I was flung to the driver's seat, breaking that window too. I remember the airbag coming out of the glove compartment very slowly, white powder everywhere as if a balloon of flour had popped. Then the car came to a stop in the muddy ditch, passenger window to the ground, and me somehow back on that side, crumpled like spilled spaghetti and my head in the mud.

In the strange new stillness, Tori Amos was singing. "I'm so sad, like a good book I can't put this day back, it's a sorta fairy-tale . . ." I would've expected her voice to be crackly or distorted, like in a movie crash scene, but she sounded perfect. A win for Ford's stereo department. With my body scrunched in the passenger seat, my mind came back online. *Wow. I think I'm OK. Am I in shock? I feel fine. Get up.*

I pushed a hand into the mud, folded my legs underneath me, and contorted myself upright. As I stood all the way up and popped my head out the driver's side window, I heard a man's voice yelling. "Don't move! Stay there!" He was walking my way from a station wagon with a woman and three kids inside.

"I'm fine, I feel fine," I said.

"OK, well, lie down!" he said as he reached me. As I finished crawling out the driver's window, I caught myself in the side-view mirror. I had blood all over my face. I guess enough adrenaline was running through me that I didn't feel shock at the sight of it. Just disconnected curiosity. I put my hand to my jaw and it felt fine, but then I touched my scalp and felt a hundred little bits of glass. When a windshield shatters, it's designed to break into tiny pieces so the shards don't stab us dead. The glass had made its home in my scalp, sending blood down my face like a *Carrie* reference. I remember thinking, *No wonder this man is worried about me, I'm a horror movie.*

I assured him I was fine, and then I heard the sirens. *That was fast,* I thought. It may not have been fast, I'm not sure. Danger collapses time into soup. The man and the station wagon disappear from my memory here.

I was surprised when a fire truck showed up. Why not an ambulance? But four or five firemen jumped out and ran over to me. They instructed me to lie on my back.

"I'm fine," I said.

"OK, let me check you," one of them said. I remember thinking he was tall and his arms were big, the muscles filling his sleeve to remove all creases. He took my foot and began squeezing me, every few inches, to see if I'd wince or if he could find a broken something. Even in my shock, I noticed how good it felt for this man to touch me. This little massage. Then I thought how pathetic it was to be thinking that, covered in blood next to a flipped, broken car.

"Am I Wolverine? Am I invincible?" I joked as the firefighter felt my neck and head.

"You must be," he said. He wasn't tender, just thorough. Which felt very masculine. Which made it more attractive.

Just then my friend Kyle's face appeared over me like a terror-struck angel. I hadn't realized we were sitting right in front of his house. Kyle had been driving home when he saw the overturned car, a car he knew to be mine. No one had ever looked at me with such horror and desperation, and I thought how nice it was that he cared that much about me.

"Everything looks fine," the firefighter said. "Do you have someone you can call to come pick you up?"

Kyle grabbed my shoulder. "How can I help? Do you want me to take you home?"

"Oh I'm OK," I said. "I'll just call my mom, she'll come get me. She'll love saving the day." Kyle handed me his phone. It was hard to see the numbers. My vision was blurry. I dialed slowly. While the phone rang, I prepared myself to sound normal. I looked around at the scene, the Explorer on its side, the huge fire truck. I thought, *Who called for this fire truck?*

"Hi, honey," she said, chipper and surprised that I'd called.

"Mom, everything's OK, but—" Something shut off my words. That horrible effect of trying to speak with tears flooding your eyes. I floated above myself, embarrassed. *You're fine. What are you losing it for? You're twenty-two years old.*

"Mom, I got in an accident," I said, my voice squeezed into the highest falsetto. "Can you come get me? I'm right by Kyle's house."

"Oh honey, I'm getting in the car. Be right there." Her voice was sturdy and ready to problem-solve.

I hung up, mortified that my friend and the firefighters had seen me cry. (I use *mortified* here on purpose. A friend realized a few years ago that the word acts as a gaydar trip wire. If you wonder if your friend is gay, ask him to tell an embarrassing story. If he says he was "mortified" when such and such a thing happened, he's gay. Straight people don't use that word.)

I don't know how long my mom took to get there. Again, it felt like she teleported. I probably joked (flirted) with the firefighters as they stood over me. Or, as I do, I began asking them about their job. "So do you often show up at car crashes? Why do you come before an ambulance?" (The reason: fire stations are distributed all over a county, unlike ERs, and time is crucial in an emergency.)

Then Mom arrived. She jumped out of the car and hurried to me. She did not have Kyle's frantic face. She was calm, if hurried. Purposeful. "Let me wipe this blood off of your face," she said, pulling a wadded-up tissue from her pocket. "You look like a horror movie. Are you OK, honey?"

I started to confidently answer, "Yes I'm fi—" and the falsetto came back. This time I didn't try to speak. It was too mortifying.

"Oh good, of course you're just fine," she said as she cleaned my face. She looked over her shoulder at the Ford. "You really did a number on that car. It says something about how safe they are. God protected you."

"I don't know why I'm crying," I choked out.

"Oh, it's OK," she said, picking glass out of my scalp. "It is scary getting in a car crash."

The firefighter stepped closer to speak. "This happens all the time," he said.

"Young men getting in car crashes?" she asked.

"No, mothers making people cry. I see it all the time. Even from fifty-year-old men."

Mom shook her head in agreement, petting my face. I felt the urge to be small and held.

I slumped into my mom's car and we drove home. I can't remember who towed the Ford Explorer, if I said bye to Kyle, if I thanked the firefighters, anything after that. I just remember Mom driving me home and saying, "We need to cook you a big meal. We need to have a *Jed's alive* celebration meal. Invite any of your friends over. What food should we cook?"

I was sitting in the front seat, touching my throat like the Little Mermaid, stunned at my inability to speak. "Beef stroganoff," I finally said, quietly. The randomness of the answer, so afield from the emotion of the crash, permitted its uttering. I was safe in the car with Mom, and the adrenaline was receding. Only then did I begin to feel that my entire body was black-and-blue.

· · ·

IN MY MIDTHIRTIES, I realized that my parents would die soon. Not like a terminal illness. I just mean in the flow of time. It hit me hardest when my mother turned seventy. I did a quick bit of math. I go home to see her twice a year. The average American woman lives to be seventy-six. If that was how it went for her, I might see my mom only twelve more times.

It is a quaking discovery to watch "Mom" becoming an old woman. Not that she looks like one. Or acts like one. Every day she seems to be on some new hike, at some new party, or laughing in a car packed with friends. But that number, seventy, has its connotations. The timeless force of nature, the mother, who exists outside of real human relationships, more an element than a person, will leave you.

I moved from Nashville to Los Angeles at nineteen and never moved back. As I became a man in my twenties and built a life of my own interests, my beliefs began to clash with hers. She was saved by Christ, the Bible her map. And I was reading books that challenged the Bible in every direction. *Guns, Germs, and Steel; Sapiens;* and *The Velvet Rage.* This complicated the time we spent together. Certain topics became live wires: Who's running for president. What the Supreme Court is doing. What the Bible does or doesn't say and mean. Best not to touch them.

I don't think I moved to California to get away from my mom, but if I interrogate my motivations, I do think I wanted to go far away to stretch out and try on different ideas and freedoms. I needed to be unwatched. And when I say unwatched, I mean by her.

But now she is in her seventies, and I am approaching forty, and I have been away from her for twenty years. And I wonder if I've been a good son. If I've chased myself at the cost of being part of a family.

That realization puts a fire into me. I decide I'm going to be intentional about making memories with her. Take some trips. Make her happy and make me feel like a good son. But I know myself. Long trips with her would be hard. There is something in me that wants to run, that doesn't want to give my mom what she wants. And what she wants is to spend time with me.

I think it has something to do with visiting home in my twenties and the guilt trip that came with any plans I made that didn't involve her. "What day can we do dinner, or a lunch?" she would ask. "Maybe we can go to a movie?" I love food and movies, but it was something about how much she wanted it. How she tried to sound like she didn't care, but I could feel the electricity, the need. And then whenever I was with her, she'd want to take pictures. Of me eating a sandwich. Of me in front of the Cracker Barrel entrance. She'd ask about my friends, listing them one by one. "How's Kenny? How's Jacob? How's my lovely Sophia?" and I would say, invariably, "They're doing great." I'd reach for any other descriptor, trying to seem engaged, pushing out words as if I needed an epidural.

Looking back, this is all very bitchy and I hate myself for it. But I'm describing a real feeling that I cannot deny. I forgive myself a little because I know we are wired for this. It is human instinct to leave the nest and go out into the world. Without that impulse, it would be too tempting to live forever with someone who cooks your food and washes your clothes and never charges you rent. We are programmed to be repulsed and run and find a mate and build a new family.

I know I'll regret it if I don't override this instinct and spend time with her. So I come up with a hack to override my claustrophobia: plan a trip and have her bring a friend.

I discovered the "bring a friend" trick a few years ago, when my mom visited Los Angeles with her friend Pam from Bible study. Pam makes my mom laugh in a way she never would with me.

They arrived at my house and Pam was already roasting her.

"Jed, you won't believe what your mother did."

"Oh be quiet, Pam," Mom yells. "Don't tell him!"

"She lost a lens out of her sunglasses and didn't notice! Walking around with one dark brown eye without a care in the world."

"PAM!" My mom is cackling and slapping her friend's shoulder.

"She had no clue, and I wonder if the woman can even see at all."

That trip showed me a different side of my mom, the one who could be someone's best friend. Pam's presence distracted her and diverted her gaze from me, and it also gave me someone else to talk to. The secret to prolonged mother-exposure was to bring a diffuser. A boomer lady friend.

A year later, my mom said it was a dream of hers to see Switzerland. "Why don't you bring a friend and we'll rent a car and drive through Switzerland, the French Alps, Austria, and Northern Italy?" I offered.

"Oh honey! Glenda has been dreaming of the same trip. Ooh, I'll call her right now."

We did that in November of 2019. Glenda is another of my mom's Bible study friends. She is as organized as a president's chief of staff. She scheduled meetings at Longhorn Steakhouse to discuss routes and activities. She sent emails detailing castles, churches, and villages. With Glenda's guidance, itineraries and train tickets and a rental car were soon booked, and directions printed out. This was very different from the way my mom and I tended to move.

Mom and I are free-flowing explorers. Less planning and more serendipity. Traveling with Glenda made everything easier and streamlined, and it also reaffirmed the "bring-a-friend" calculation. Without Glenda to compare ourselves to, I wouldn't have felt a cute companionship with my mother as we planned the trip. I wouldn't have said, "Runs in the family, doesn't it?"

We flew into Munich and picked up our rental car. "Oh look at your hair, it's gorgeous," my mom said to the tired man behind the Hertz desk. "I believe you should tell people nice things if you think 'em. And your hair is thick and shiny and beautiful."

His head jerked back and his blank DMV face popped open to a smile. "How would you like to be upgraded to a BMW?" he asked.

"A luxury car?!"

"Yes."

She turned to me and Glenda. "The Lord surprises us, doesn't He. A sign!"

We walked out to a BMW station wagon and put our bags in the back. As we climbed in, I realized I'd forgotten that one of the key thefts of age is your ability to get up and down. The car's belly basically dragged on the ground—great for tight curves through the mountains, but hard for an aging body to get in and out of. Mom stood in front of the open door, planning her descent. She grabbed the handle on the ceiling, threw one leg in, and then pulled at the handle to guide her downward, swinging her butt into the seat with a thud. Grunting all the way like she was throwing bags of cement. "This is going to be a workout!" Mom laughed.

"We can do it Barbara," Glenda said, readying herself to get in the backseat. "We're representing boomers everywhere!"

We drove from Munich up to the Matterhorn, where the ladies bought elaborate cuckoo clocks, then down to Rapallo, Italy, for a night on the Mediterranean. I'd never touched that sea before, so I woke up early and walked down to the pebbled beach alone. It was cloudy and quiet. Doing something by myself for the first time in days got me reflecting on our vacation. This trip was "for" my mom. Performing my job as a good son. Insurance against regret. I was having fun with her and Glenda, and I felt good for making this trip happen. But I walked alone across the pebbled beach thinking, "Why must everything be *for* something? When I was a kid, I explored to explore. To know what was over there. Not *because* of anything."

I wondered about my friendship with my mom. Is it friendship? How can it be? Friendship is chosen. Friendship is discovered. But a mother and a son have a bond that is necessary. If the son exists, the mother exists. She may have abandoned him, she may have abused him, she may have loved him and laughed with him. But no matter what, there is a relation that must be accounted for. So how could it be friendship? What does friendship with a parent mean?

The trip felt good in a purposeful way. Thinking of my mom's joy. Of Glenda's joy. And I could slip a few things in there just for me. Like this moment, dipping a toe in the Mediterranean. My weird son-flight instinct seemed to demand an experience that was just for me.

I walked back and found the happy ladies drinking coffee in the restaurant café. "Where to today, Jeddypoo?" Mom said.

We drove from there into Austria, where puffy snow was dumping everywhere, and back up into Germany. All the way Mom was light and full of wonder—that is to say, she was very fun. It made me feel foolish for pre-deciding that this trip would be hard. Every turn on every road, she would say, "This is a once-in-a-lifetime opportunity."

"It's more beautiful than the pitchers," Glenda would add, her Southern accent transforming the word *picture*. "Quick, let's make a pitcher!"

In a small village in southern Germany, my mom flung open the window of our hotel and cried out to the ringing bell tower, "I feel like I'm in *Beauty and the Beast*." Every cobblestone was a miracle. Every bakery. The different license plates. The bubble sirens of police cars. "Isn't this wonderful!?"

"We would be lost at every intersection without you, Jed," Glenda said.

On the Bernina Express, a train that crosses the Alps from Switzerland to Italy, the ladies could've powered a steam engine with their gasps. "Nature's beauty warms my heart," my mom said as if to no one, hands crossed over her heart, looking at the snow-covered pine trees with Glenda sitting next to her.

I was lost in the moment, listening to the gentle clucking of their conversation, when my mom snapped her fingers at me. "Oh Jed, there's the best new movie with my favorite actor, Shee-yuh . . ." A pause of doubt that she's getting the name wrong. "It's called *Peanut Butter Falcon*. Have you seen it?"

"Your favorite actor, who?" I asked, smiling.

"Oh what's his name. Shayuh Buhl-e-off? No . . ."

"I don't know who you're talking about," I said, lying.

"Oh yes you do. He's a big deal. He's in lots of movies. Shee Labioff?"

"No idea."

"It's not Beowulf, ugh . . ." She puts on her glasses and starts googling. "Shayuh Labeoff! That's it."

"Are you meaning to say Shia LaBeouf?" I said, grinning like the Grinch.

"That's it!! I'm such a goose. Meme always called me a goose."

"A goose? Why?"

"Because I'm just like a goose, I wake up in a new world every day."

An image of my mom as a teenager appeared. Peppy and pretty. My meme, her mother, snapping at her, annoyed at her prettier daughter floating through life. My mom, a teen girl, internalizing her mother's insults.

We came home from the trip glowing, and I was proud that I'd made time to do it. Of course I documented the trip on Instagram, because my mom's Southern accent and jovial gooseness makes people happy. I got loads of messages, like, "I want to do this with my mom, you make it look so fun." "I hope my son wants to do this with me when he's grown up, he certainly doesn't want to right now." I learned that it is not normal to travel solo with a parent.

Mom and Glenda were already planning the next trip. They wanted to do New Zealand. Fall of 2020. Perfect. I said I was in.

Of course, 2020 swatted our dreams like everyone else's. I thought, "Finally, something that will bring us all together, a global pandemic, a shared event that will restore social capital to America!" And maybe we had that for five or seven days, when we were banging pots and pans on the patio.

But alas, soon everything is a mess. Chinese bioterrorism, vaccine computer chips, government overreach, and child abuse. The bifurcation may be worse than ever. And I am stuck in my home, far from my seventy-something parents, and they don't seem to care about the disease. Life is normal in Nashville. My mom is at

the fair, at a packed church, at her granddaughter's recital. My dad
sends me videos of himself licking his fingers at a barbecue place,
to show just how free he is. I picture them getting sick. Will I be
allowed to see them at the hospital? Will I have to say goodbye
over FaceTime? I've seen those scenarios in the news and I'm
haunted by them.

So now our political realities become different planets. California believes. Tennessee doesn't. And I'm sitting in LA worrying
that my parents are going to die, and there's a little anger in there
because it'll be their own damn fault. I want to fly home and spend
time with them. But what if I hand-deliver the virus that kills
them?

This horrible moment in history is keeping me from my parents in the precious golden years of their life. The claustrophobia
of time constricting again.

In the fall of 2020, after we've let go of New Zealand, Mom
has another idea. She calls me. "Jed, you know how we always
wanted to go on a European cruise together? I found one."

"Oh wow, when?!"

"It's in a year, November 2021. The Covid stuff will be over by
then. It starts in Venice, Italy, and ends in Israel!"

"That sounds incredible."

"OK, Jed, hear me out," her tone changes to concern.

"Uh-oh."

"Don't make a judgment yet. It's a Glenn Beck cruise."

"Mother!"

"It's called Cruise Thru History. You travel and discuss the
foundations of faith and roots of democracy. The tour looks incredible. And, take it from me, Glenn Beck is one of the most

passionate history buffs I've ever seen. A trip like this would be great fodder for future articles, podcasts, books. The education would last a lifetime."

"Mom, a Glenn Beck CRUISE!?"

"Just think about it. It would be powerful. And then the trip ends with Glenn interviewing Bill O'Reilly in Israel."

"I'm sweating," I say.

"I'm sure Glenda or Pam will want to come. I'll pay for you to go. It's expensive but a once-in-a-lifetime opportunity."

"OK, let me think about it."

We hang up and I am picturing a boat full of conservative boomers. I imagine sitting through lectures that make me want to sink the ship. But my mom is not wrong. This would be fun to write about. And I picture my mom meeting a man there and falling in love. I picture me, meeting some waiter who is stuck serving all these people and smoking cigarettes with him at 1 A.M. I picture having real quality time with my mom. I text her that I'll go.

She pays for the tickets in full. And I get excited to be a tourist with my mom, a voyeur, a social anthropologist.

But Covid doesn't float away. And then 2021 rolls in and we get vaccines. Well, some of us do. Many conservatives don't want the Fauci Ouchie. And Italy won't let anyone in without the vaccine. Neither will Israel. There is no way this cruise is happening.

But now I really want it to.

Months roll by. "Mom, is the cruise gonna happen?"

"I'm not sure. I haven't heard anything from them."

"They aren't updating you? The cruise company?"

"Nothing."

"You already paid them thousands of dollars. I'd think they'd be sending you constant updates about the situation."

"Me too. I've been emailing them with questions. I'm going to ask for a refund soon. I'm keeping a paper trail."

More months pass. We're now two months away from the trip. No communication from the cruise company. Italy is still not accepting the unvaccinated. Covid is still rampant. Mom sends a dramatic email to customer service: "I'm a poor old woman in her seventies, and I've spent my savings on this trip. I can't afford to lose this money!"

A week later, her credit card is refunded. No confirmation email. No acknowledgment.

The cruise isn't happening, but I've blocked off those days in November, and I want to go on a trip with my mom.

We both love a road trip. And I don't want my mom flying during the pandemic if I can avoid it, so . . . maybe I can fly to her and take her somewhere. Maybe somewhere in the West? And then I think: my mom's great walk across America, the three-year trek she made with my father in the '70s.

From 1976 to 1979, my mom and dad walked 2,600 miles from Louisiana to the Oregon Coast. My dad started the walk in New York. He ambled for two years to New Orleans, where he met my mother. They fell in love, got married, and then set out together for the Pacific Ocean. News of their big adventure became a national sensation. They appeared on the cover of *National Geographic.* They wrote books about the trip that sold twelve million copies. They were young, in love, and famous. My mom started the walk at age twenty-seven and ended it at thirty-one. She did this iconic feat before I existed.

We could retrace her steps. She could guide me through her memories. I would get to see her as she was in her late twenties. Maybe understanding her then would help me understand us now.

When I floated the idea, she was keen.

"I'll start collecting all my notes and journals," she said. And that she did. Soon she was sending me photos of a binder she made, with printed maps and highlighted routes and unpublished photos. And her journal from the walk, which I didn't know existed. The little book was full to the brim with her thoughts as a young woman, newly married, on foot across this country. "I even took notes of my fights with your dad," she said, showing me her thick journal on FaceTime. Flipping through the pages, there was an entry for every day. It was a play-by-play document of their first years of marriage. A love story where I'd never known the plot, only the end. The story that led to me.

Growing up, I rarely heard her speak about it. She'd mention "the Walk" and talk about missing Colorado, or stare a little too long at a Christmas card from Texas or Oregon. I'd complain about mowing the lawn and she'd snap back, "I walked three thousand miles with a fifty-pound backpack. You can ride on a mower with your Walkman." When she did mention it, there was a quickness, passing over it as if implying, "No further questions." After the books, after having three kids together, her relationship with my dad fell apart. They divorced. Bitterly. And the public memory of the great Walk Across America became his story more than hers.

I heard bits of it through the years. The chosen parts. Stories that planted her flag in the journey, proof that she was there in spite of my father's fame. She slid off a glacier in Colorado and was saved only when her backpack hooked onto a shard of ice at the cliff. She was hit by a car while walking through Salt Lake and launched forty feet onto the lawn of a mortuary. She spent a night in a field, hiding from drunks threatening to rape her. I heard her say these things, but as a kid, then as a teenager, I had no reference for the extraordinary. Maybe every parent had stories like this?

In my adulthood I have realized that it is not normal to have parents who walked across America, who wrote books that people still remember, who've been on the covers of magazines. And I've never really talked to my mom about it. I've never imagined her young and in love and crossing the American West on foot for three years.

Cosmically, a mother is different than a father. Her body grew you, nursed you. Your cells built by her cells. Beyond that, my mother was the one who raised me. My parents divorced when I was too young to remember, and she got custody. I spent weekends with my father. He let me ride in the back of the truck to the Sonic drive-in and let me get whatever I wanted. My mother sat by the bed each night and said a prayer with her hand on my heart. My dad let me watch R-rated movies. My mom spanked me and helped me (the best she could) with my science projects. My dad was my friend. My mom was my mom.

Not long ago, maybe two years ago, I was visiting my dad at his farm in Tennessee. We were walking through the wood frame of his new house under construction. I think we were talking about high ceilings or fireplace mantels, and he said, "Jed, just so you know, when you get married, to a guy I mean, I'll be happy to walk you down the aisle."

The statement came from nowhere, with no lead-in. I snapped alert like a rabbit, quiet and listening. He must've been thinking about that for a long time. He must have made a plan to tell me, not wanting to make it too much of a show. Just lob it in while we were doing something else, to keep the moment from becoming sentimental.

I felt his awkwardness at the sincerity, so I said thank you and nothing more. But inside I was expanding like a shockwave. A permission I hadn't exactly expected—and, for fear of the alternative, never asked for.

He moved on. "I got this wood beam from the old red shack at the front of the farm. It must be from the 1800s. It'll make a great mantel."

"Wow, that is so cool. It's beautiful. I love the chipped paint," I said, my mind flooded with warmth.

But my mom? No. That endorsement will never come.

Well, I assume no. Two of the things that we "can't talk about" are the inerrancy of the Bible and her belief that my sexuality is not God's desire for my life. These are two things I do not believe.

I've thought about my future wedding, many times. About the "best" day of my life. Will she refuse to attend? Will she sit there and stew? Will she come around and celebrate my union? It's too much to worry about. In my mind, I've already mitigated the pain by resolving to not invite her. Not any family, really. To elope, or do some little camping-trip-slash-wedding with friends in Big Sur. That way we can go wild, do mushrooms, and drink without a disapproving gaze. Edit out the complexity. Avoid. I'm good at that.

But I realize that's not what I really want. I want her there, crying because she's moved by love. Crying that her baby boy found a man who loves him right. Crying at how proud she is. I want that more than anything.

My mother and I have spoken about my sexuality only a few times. I came out to her when I was twenty. She said she loved me unconditionally, but she would pray that God would heal me and deliver to me an attraction to women. On that point I agreed with her. I hoped, too.

We didn't speak of it again until I was twenty-seven. By then, my wish to change had grown brittle and flaked away. Day by day, I'd grown more confident that I was exactly as God intended: a gay man. I don't even remember how the phone call went, but I think I had defended being gay in a Facebook post and said the popular Bible interpretations were wrong, and she wasn't happy about that. All I really remember is that she called homosexuality "disgusting" and I hung up on her.

The next time it came up, I was thirty-five. I'd talked about her in a podcast interview, and she felt bullied. The tone of the interview was "You must be so brave to be in a relationship with a woman like her." Which, upon reflection, feels unfair. She emailed me in a tone I didn't recognize. Angry. Terse. Sterile. And it was clear that her thinking had not changed.

Reading that email, something snapped in me. *Thirty-five years old, and she can still twist my guts like this? She can still make me feel tiny?* I started typing. I wrote her the email to end all emails. For the first time, I spelled out exactly what I believed and why. I was tired of tiptoeing. I'd had my first kiss, my first boyfriend, my first sex . . . all monumental moments in my life, and I couldn't talk to my mom about it. I'd brought more than one boyfriend back to Nashville and introduced him to her as my friend. I was tired of maneuvering my life around this woman, of doing or not doing things for fear of how she could make me feel. So I snapped and wrote it out: "I am gay and that is not changing . . . I love my sexuality and believe God made me this way . . . I will one day have a husband and your beliefs will prevent us from spending holidays with you." My fingers fumed as I typed.

I hit Send and immediately worried that I'd made a mistake. That I'd said too much.

After an excruciating few days, she wrote back. "You've given me a lot to think about. I love you, Jeddypoo." Whoa. That felt big to me. Just a little wiggle room. Maybe a crack in the wall.

From there, time passed and she never wrote again. I would test her with one-off comments. A mention of a gay men's camping trip. A bad date referenced in passing. No specifics. Just the date's existence, to see if she bristled. And she did not. She was silent, but perhaps silence was a sign of acquiescence.

I WONDERED IF FINALLY, after all of that, she was coming around. Maybe if she saw me happy and in love, something would shift. Maybe if she met him, knew him, the concept of "homosexuality" would be crushed by the specificity of a human she cares about.

What if, by pre-deciding that she'll say no, I'm missing the opportunity for my mom to give me away to my husband? How could she not want to celebrate my love at that point?

But what if she does say no?

I decide I'm a weak idiot and I need to ask her, somewhere on this road trip. Us, trapped in the car. I can't keep ignoring it, like a broken smoke detector out of reach. I'd rather know than wonder.

But when, exactly? How do I bring it up? I'm not sure. Even thinking about it, psyching myself up, has me squirming.

Her power.

This may be one of the most fundamental concerns of my generation, or any: How do I stay in a relationship with family when differences push us apart? What do I do when our disagreements feel so fundamental, so consequential? The internet is rich with discussions on boundaries, ditching toxic people, and choosing mental peace. Every holiday season, I see no less than a thousand memes about people not wanting to go home. The unshakable bond of blood turns out to be quite shakable.

But a mother's influence is difficult to disenthrall. It is not like the scorching sun. You cannot shade yourself from it. It is more enveloping and inescapable, like air.

2

. . .

WE PACK THE CAR the night before leaving. My mother has a Nissan Murano SUV. It's cream colored, and it is a convertible.

Have you ever seen an SUV convertible? Most people haven't, because I've noticed how they stop and gawk. The vehicle looks like a joke. It sits high off the road, and it has only two doors, with a backseat the size of a sock drawer. The front seats try to be high-tech. They don't just slide up quick with a lever when you need to get in the back. You push a button and wait while they inch forward and fold at the pace of a tectonic plate. The doors are so huge, so long, that to open them or pull them shut requires hulk-like strength. And the trunk . . . well, it can only fit a carry-on, because the cloth top has to fit in there, too. Nissan stopped making the model in 2014, because they are terribly designed.

But I will tell you something, this car with the top down is a lucious experience. You are high off the pavement and open to the sky. Superior. And no one looking at you knows that every other design feature is as functional as snowshoes on a dance floor. A friend recently told me that these Muranos are collector's items now. There are entire online forums with people obsessed.

Mom and I cram her suitcase into the trunk and put mine in the backseat. This will be our vessel, to follow the exact path she walked forty-four years ago to Florence, Oregon. Our journey will be a massive loop: Nashville to New Orleans to Florence and back to Nashville. Five thousand five hundred miles in total.

We don't have a hard deadline or people to see. Almost everyone from her walk is dead or lost. But I will see the landscapes my mother walked through. And hopefully, by putting her in those landscapes, with her journal in her hand, I'll see her as she was.

As we climb in to leave, I notice Mom has put a big fabric cooler in the backseat, the kind you might take to a picnic. "What's in this bag, Mother?"

"Oh, in this bag," she says like a QVC presenter, "I have water, vitamins, and sweets, all the essentials." She unzips it. "I've got some apples if you wanna be really healthy, but I've got all this Halloween candy, and—"

She pulls up a big plastic bag. "Look at this. Look. At. This."

It holds two apples and twenty pounds of candy.

"Is it the good stuff or the cheap stuff?"

"No, it's the good stuff. We've got Snickers, Twix, M&M's. Grab some!"

"Not ready for candy just yet," I say. It is 8 A.M.

I start the car and pull out of the driveway. Only now, seeing her sitting beside me, situating herself and buckling up, do I notice that I've forgotten my rule: when traveling with Mom, have her bring a friend. The great diffuser. Whoops. It's just me and her. For the next however long.

This is going to be brutal.

We've planned to get to New Orleans in one haul, no sightseeing. Nashville-to-New-Orleans wasn't on Mom's walk route, so there's no history to revisit. We're moving, but this day feels like prep.

She fishes in her purse and pulls out a white-and-blue contraption about the size of a pack of cigarettes. It looks like a spray bottle, or a taser. "Let's take a hit of my bong to get us going," she says.

When Mom says "bong," she means her nebulizer. It turns water into vapor, and she huffs it all day like a singer breathing hot mist before a performance. Except Mom's machine is handheld. I'm surprised she doesn't carry it in a gun sling.

But my mom is not just inhaling water. "Let's get some colloidal silver in those lungs," she says.

Second to prayer, colloidal silver is Mom's insurance policy on life. She makes her own, soaking two silver rods in a glass vat of water that sits next to her kitchen sink. I'll let her explain it. This is from one of her emails telling me how to live forever: "I use distilled water and 99% pure silver rods. The rods are connected to a positive and negative charge (think of a jumper cable for your car) and they are immersed in the distilled water. Some people leave the rods in the water 2–4 hours. I leave mine in for 8–12 hours so my silver water is extra strength and powerful . . . I drink ¼ cup colloidal silver in a glass of water before bed, and have for years and years. RARELY am I ever sick. I take a bottle of colloidal silver on every trip (especially overseas) in case I pick up a stomach bug or am around anyone who is sick. I use it on wounds, use it for pink eye, ear infections, the flu, and more because it kills over 600 viruses and most bacteria, including MRSA. There are also studies that show the benefits of colloidal silver against cancer."

Every time I'm home, she gives me a bottle of the stuff to take back to Los Angeles. I, like a good millennial, googled its effectiveness. The scientific establishment seems to believe that colloidal silver does approximately nothing good, and in large quantities, some bad. Perhaps you've seen the viral meme of the old blue man? He consumed so much colloidal silver that his skin dyed blue from the inside. He looks like a Smurf with a white beard. Well, he looked like a Smurf. He's dead. Maybe from something common like heart failure, but . . .

When I told my mother this, she wouldn't hear it. "I know it works. I've been using it for years. I don't care what those articles say. I've read hundreds of articles about it."

"Yeah, but which articles? Who's writing them?"

"I never get sick. That's all the evidence I need."

It's true, my mother is in fantastic health. She has the energy of a thirty-year-old. This does not help my case.

She holds the little contraption up to her mouth, inhales for four seconds, then exhales with karate volume. She hands it to me. "Get this deep into your lungs. Inhale all the way down. This is how we start the trip, fighting viruses and healthy and prayed up."

I push the little button and breathe the vapor. It has no flavor and feels like nothing.

"OK, now that we're protected, let's get McDonald's," she says. "Let's start with a treat."

McDonald's is a must on any road trip with my mom. When I was a kid, she couldn't afford plane tickets or hotels for her three kids, so we drove places. We went to national parks towing a crusty pop-up camper with duct tape patching the screens. Mom would crank up the camper, plug everything in, make up our beds, cook us dinner. Only as I write this am I realizing how much work that was. And how we never helped her. She just let us run off to explore the creek or the woods. But on those trips, we always ate McDonald's breakfast. Mom referred to it as a *treat,* the word pregnant with notions of bad behavior and indulgence and also something earned. My order was an Egg McMuffin with sausage. Heavenly. Those food scientists really nailed the meat, the bread and cheese, that rubbery egg made in that tiny skillet. Whatever Wiccan devil worship they practiced to perfect that spell on my taste buds, it worked.

We drive straight to McDonald's and I order said treat. "You know they use real eggs," Mom says, protesting too much.

My mom opts for a sausage biscuit with coffee and hash browns. She is incapable of not getting the whole meal deal because the word *deal* is in the name. My whole life she's come home with her arms full of TJ Maxx clothes, saying, "This was marked down from eighty-five dollars!"

"Mom, it's not a deal if you don't need it and weren't going to buy it."

"Oh yes it is."

She hands her hash brown to me, "Here, you eat this, I can't eat all this."

"Then why'd you order it? I don't want it."

"You're growing, yes you do."

"I'm thirty-eight years old," I say. "I'm not growing in any direction that I want to."

She never seems to understand my eating habits. Whenever

I'm home in Nashville, she offers to make me breakfast every day. It is her way of finding guaranteed time together, of having a morning routine with me, and I always accept her offer. "Eggs, bacon, toast?" she asks when I walk into the kitchen. Or, "Rice and peanut butter?" My grandfather ate that almost every morning—a Depression-era stopgap—and it tastes like sugary nostalgia.

"No bread," I say, trying to explain my diet. "I'm trying to cut bread out. It's not good for me. And no cheese. I'm for sure lactose intolerant."

"No cheese on the eggs? Just eggs and bacon? Not even one piece of toast?"

"No."

"An English muffin, then?"

"No."

"What about fruit? No cheese at all in the eggs?"

"Fruit is OK. But no cheese."

"OK fine." Then she stirs the eggs in the bowl in a way that says, *I'm making food for a madman.*

For her, there is a right way to make breakfast. It involves butter, bread, and cheese. Remove any one of them, and you are not making food. You're making California propaganda flavorless cardboard. But she makes the most delicious eggs. She whips them French style, meaning constant movement, low heat, and taking them out of the pan earlier than you'd think. And they are damn good with cheese. I get why the loss of that flavor is hard for her. Her eggs are never dry. They're fluffy. I think she puts milk in them, but she doesn't mention that, for fear I'll say no. The eggs come to the table with cheese. "Just a little."

The last time I was home, she walked in showing off gluten-free bread, displaying it like a *Price Is Right* model. I was legitimately touched. That's all a child wants from a parent sometimes, to be taken seriously.

As we pull out of McDonald's, I hold up my phone and film her in the passenger seat. "OK Mom, what are we doing?" Whenever I film her, she speaks with a put-on radio voice that isn't her actual voice. "Well, this is our very first day on our road trip across America." There's giddy excitement in her tone. "Retracing the actual trail your dad and I walked across America from 1976 to 1979. We're gonna start in New Orleans, where I was working on a master's degree at the New Orleans Baptist Theological Seminary. And we were married at Word of Faith Temple."

"Do you think it's still there?"

"Yes."

"We're gonna find it."

"Yes. And when we left, we left at three o'clock in the morning on July the Fourth, 19 and 76."

"Here we come, New Orleans," I say.

We reach the interchange for I-65. There is one sign pointing south to Huntsville and another pointing north to downtown Nashville. The spelled-out word reminds me of my mom's dog, also named Nashville, a nine-year-old Havanese with short legs and a floofy broom-brush tail.

It dawns on me that I am home and Nash isn't there. He was killed earlier this year. A family member drove over him with their truck in the driveway. It was Nashville's fault. Mom's favorite thing to say about him was that "he has no sense." And he didn't. Somehow, maybe he saw a squirrel, maybe he heard a sound and lost focus, he waddled right under the tire as the truck was backing up.

My mom was miserable when it happened. Mourning the little friend who spent most of his life at her feet. But now it had been six months and she didn't seem sad anymore.

"I miss Nash," I say. "Are you going to get another dog?"

"No. Not right now."

"I don't like you in that house alone all the time."

"Well I do. I like not worrying about anyone pissing on my oriental rugs. I like being able to just pick up and leave whenever I want. I don't have to worry about nothin'. I'm enjoying it. I'll get a dog when I stop traveling."

When I stop traveling. I shiver. She's already making plans. I hate the thought and I know it's on its way. Around which bend in the road? The next one? A few away? Seventy-four is a funny age, because some people live to be a hundred, and twenty-six years is a long time. But lots of people only live to be seventy-five.

I hope she'll get another dog. I like her having something to be mad at, something to talk to, something to complain about. A little resistance training makes the muscles strong. A little cussing at the dog keeps the mind alive.

Not that my mom is just sitting in that house alone. Her calendar is stuffed with Bible studies and weekly excursions with her friends across the mid-South. The Boomer Moms, as they call themselves. Every Wednesday they pile into one of their cars and head on some little jaunt. A historic German settlement in Kentucky. An antiques mall. A waterfall in McMinnville.

In high school, I noticed that my mom wasn't like a lot of my friends' parents. She was social. Booked up and popular. But when I spent time at friends' houses, doing sleepovers and Nintendo 64 GoldenEye tournaments, the parents were always there. Silent and upstairs, or puttering in the kitchen. As far as I could tell, they went to work, and then they came home. They didn't have ladies over, whispering in the kitchen about someone's daughter's divorce. Or laughing as they walked out the door to a Friday night movie. "Do your parents have friends?" I asked once at a sleepover. "No, they just hang out with each other. Or watch TV."

But day trips and get-togethers still leave Mom alone in that house at night. The only sound is conservative talk radio. It's on when she wakes up, and it's on when she goes to bed. "Mom, do you listen to this poison all day?" I asked her once, standing in the kitchen. "I have it on so that Nash has something to listen to when I'm out running errands," she explained. But now Nash is dead, and the radio still plays. It's just her and Glenn Beck, her and Sean Hannity, her and Clay Travis, the guy who took over for Rush Limbaugh. Filling the house with the emergency of a collapsing America.

Who knows, maybe Nash chose to jump under that tire.

Whenever I go home to Nashville, I step into an alternate universe where American values are under attack. Where no one can pray in schools anymore. Where Biden is the biggest liar since Obama. It's not just that I don't agree with the worldview. It's that to actually hear those voices droning all day—the things they're saying, how angry and scary they are to me—it makes me sad to think my mom agrees with them. My sweet mother. My rock of unconditional love. I'm sure she would say the same about the journalism I consume. *It attacks family values. It belittles real Americans. It celebrates the murder of the unborn. It attacks marriage. It hates God. It relishes in hating conservatives.*

A month or two before our trip, we're sitting in the living room watching Netflix. She has two recliners on either side of the fireplace pointed to the TV. Our Olivia Colman movie has ended, and I turn on the first docuseries I see, about a string of murders around Times Square in the 1970s. Within the first ten minutes, I realize that the entire cast of interviewees are sex workers. They explain how sex work was disparaged and looked down on in the '70s, unlike today when it's a job as legitimate as being a firefighter.

We're not even looking at the TV at this point. I'm deep on Instagram or Twitter while my mom flips through her phone. But ten minutes in, she says, "Want me to turn it off? I don't like this."

"I'm not ready for bed," I say. "I'll keep watching it. Well, I'm not really watching it, it's on in the background."

"This kind of glorification. It's wrong," she says, getting up out of her chair. "It's an abomination in the Bible."

"So is eating shrimp," I say, annoyed and sharp. She doesn't retort. I almost wish she had, because now I feel mean. She just let me be a smart-ass, and now she's walking to bed. "Good night, honey," she says, shifting to a kind tone.

"Good night, sweet Mama," I say, shifting too.

I tell you all of this because we're on a road trip now, and I want you to feel how hard it is to choose something to listen to. As we speed down I-65, I decide to give NPR a try. I hold my phone up at the top of the steering wheel and click *Up First*, their daily news podcast. I listen to it almost every morning. I know Mom is skeptical of the mainstream media, but the news feels safe, and NPR tries to be balanced. At least I think it does. I know my dad sometimes listens to it, and he's full-on conservative too.

First is a Covid update. It's Rob Stein, telling us that 86 percent of seniors are vaccinated, including 80 percent of Republicans in that age group. His voice has a lisp that makes him sound cute. Approachable. He tells us that nine out of ten deaths are happening among the unvaccinated. Next up, the abortion ban in Texas.

The Supreme Court is listening to a challenge on the state's use of bounty hunters to enforce the law.

"Can we turn this off?" she says. "I don't like listening to this."

"The news?" I ask.

"Yes, I don't want to hear it."

"OK, yeah, it's depressing." I hit Pause. My mind buzzes with terms like "liberal agenda" and whatever else I assume she believes. Here I am, wondering what I can listen to in front of my mother in her own car. Most of my podcasts are too progressive, in ways I don't even notice when I'm by myself. But with her, I hear them differently. They'll say something about Trump, or Fox News, or structural racism, or trans athletes, and I'll assume she's bristling. Or she'll just listen a little too closely, analyzing, and I won't be able to think clearly, both listening and also listening for her. I wonder what I love that she would love, too. We could put on music, but she somehow hears every lyric. Lyrics I've never registered or noticed. I'll never forget the time she asked, "What is skeet?"

I scan my regular consumptions—*New York Times,* Vox, NPR, *Radiolab, This American Life,* Sam Harris, *Popcast,* Esther Perel—not one of the people on these shows will say Jesus is Lord. Not one of them will say America is a "shining city on a hill." Not one will blame Black on Black violence on a fatherless generation.

All day I hear voices discussing climate change, structural racism, entrenched power dynamics, oppressed classes, identity categories trapping populations in poverty, ableism, decolonizing fitness, nonmonogamy, the joy of gay sex, sex-positivity, on and on. And it's not even that I agree with every position taken by my chosen voices, it's that their basic worldview and their perspective on the project of society is similar to mine, so I listen with charity and understanding. Of course, I'm a hypocrite. I ask for the grace of nuance for myself and don't give it to my mother. I assume she agrees with all of her madmen.

"So what do you want to listen to?" I ask.

"Let's learn about Princess Diana or some murder show or something true crime," she says. "Ooh, I saved a couple that looked great, lemme look 'em up." Her voice is upbeat. She is used to my sounding frustrated, and she never meets my tone. She counters it with brightness, positivity.

She fiddles with her phone, glasses down her nose, her crooked pointer finger scrolling through God knows what. I cannot see what she's doing because she has a privacy screen on her phone. I have no idea who she thinks is trying to eavesdrop on her. The back of her phone also has a thick sticker with a swirling symbol resembling an atom. It is her 5G-blocking radiation protection sticker. It costs $20. I know because she bought me one.

I notice my phone in my crotch. I always put it there unconsciously. Now that I've noticed it, it is hot from running Google Maps. I wonder if it's cooking my testicles. My phone does not bear the sticker.

"OK, we can listen to *You're Wrong About: Princess Diana*," she says, "or one about 'the greatest unsolved plane hijacking of all time: D. B. Cooper.'"

You're Wrong About? That podcast is two liberal women cussing up a storm. I'm surprised my mom likes it.

"Wow, OK. Let's listen to the hijacker," I say. "I've never heard of that." It feels good to be on the same page, excited about something together.

A friendly male voice narrates. I'm picturing a white-haired man sitting at a desk covered in papers and open books and a microphone.

This is the true story of the greatest unsolved plane hijacking of all time. On November 24, 1971, Dan Cooper boarded Northwest Orient Airlines Flight 305 bound for Seattle from Portland. He was wearing a dark suit and black tie. The man purchased his airline ticket under the name Dan Cooper, but because of a news flub, he became known in the cultural consciousness as D. B. Cooper.

Once in the air, Cooper handed a note to Florence Schaffner, the flight attendant. She thought it was just from a lonely businessman giving her his number, so she dropped it unopened into her purse. Cooper leaned close to her and whispered, "Miss, you'd better look at that note. I have a bomb."

Mom and I glance at each other and smile. "We need more hijackings!" I say, and don't know why I said it.

The note directed the flight attendant to sit down next to Cooper. She asked to see the bomb and he opened the case and she saw long red cylinders that looked like dynamite. Cooper closed the briefcase and handed Schaffner his demands: $200,000 in "negotiable American currency," four parachutes, and a fuel truck standing by in Seattle to refuel the aircraft upon arrival. Schaffner delivered the note to the pilots and when she returned, he was wearing dark sunglasses.

The thirty-five other passengers were told that their arrival in Seattle would be delayed because of a "minor mechanical difficulty." Northwest Orient's president authorized payment of the ransom and ordered all employees to cooperate fully with the hijacker. The aircraft circled Puget Sound for almost two hours while Seattle police and the FBI assembled the parachutes and ransom money. Schaffner described Cooper as calm, polite, and well-spoken. Another flight attendant, Tina Mucklow, said, "He wasn't nervous. He seemed rather nice. He was never cruel or nasty. He was thoughtful and calm all the time." When Mucklow asked Cooper if he had a grudge against the airline, he replied, "I don't have a grudge against your airline, Miss. I just have a grudge."

"Oh this show is wonderful," Mom says. "I love history and mystery."

The plane landed in Seattle, and Cooper was given the $200,000 cash, the equivalent of about $1.3 million today. He took his four parachutes and demanded food for the crew before releasing all the passengers. With three pilots and one flight attendant, they took off heading south. He asked to be flown to Mexico City. Shortly after takeoff, he tied the bank bag full of $20 bills to his body and put on one of the parachutes. Somewhere north of Portland, he jumped into the night.

The case became a national sensation. The FBI followed thousands of leads and wound up empty-handed, without even a hunch as to D. B. Cooper's true identity.

Then, eight years after the hijacking, a clue. On February 10, 1980, a family having a picnic on the shores of the Columbia River near Vancouver, Washington, stumbled across three rotted packets of $20 bills totaling $5,800. They were buried in an odd spot, about fifty feet from the water's edge. The search area had been eighteen miles downstream, outside of the designated flight path. Cooper must've buried the money here, right? But why? Why wouldn't he have brought it with him?

The FBI has remained fairly certain that Cooper didn't survive the jump. For several reasons: He wasn't trained for a jump like that. He landed in a dense, tall forest. And most specifically, none of the ransom money, besides that found on the river, has ever turned up. Meaning it was unlikely to have been spent.

But who buried it upriver? The crime remains the only unsolved case of air piracy in commercial aviation history. The FBI officially suspended the investigation in 2016.

I look over at my mom. She clasps her hands and grunts, "Ooh this is great!" It feels good to share the joy of this podcast with her. For once I'm not listening with a double mind, wondering if she's bristling at something I take for granted. We're united in our relish.

We cross the Alabama state line, turn west at Birmingham, and drive into Mississippi. Near the Louisiana border we pass a billboard that says, "Hell is real. Are you ready to meet your maker?" I remember when I believed in hell. Now that feeling is so distant. It feels silly now. To believe that God, who rigged the whole show, who wrote every day of our lives in a book before one came to be, could make us, knowing we'll sin and not repent, and burn. And that somehow, it's our fault. Reality can be cruel. A good family can die from a tree branch falling on their car. A hippo can kill a baby gazelle for fun. Why make the system so mean when the random mess of disease and death is cruel enough?

I wince as I write these things because I know my mom will read these words. I hesitate to say what I really believe, because she is so invested in my believing what she believes. She prays every day, every single day, for me to give my life back to Jesus. "I just really think if you read the Bible, you'd understand. If you really dug into the Word."

"Mom, I've read that whole book. I spent my entire teens and twenties wrestling with it." I want to keep talking—*and it's horrible, and made up, and a tool of oppression and delusion, and perhaps evil!*—but I don't say that. I would rather let it float in ambiguity, to keep her happy. To keep her hope alive.

But she is open and bold about her beliefs, even if they hurt me. Why can't I be the same? Why can't I stand in my truth as she stands in hers? If my truth hurts her, well, the truth is what it is. And God knows her truth hurts me. Isn't being true to our convictions the most loving thing we can do? We're both locked in a stalemate of certainty: We both believe "I am right and the other is deceived. They are trapped in a labyrinth of lies. I am liberated."

The car moves southwest in silence. Mom is quiet in the passenger seat, deep in her phone.

"Look what I just posted," she says, holding up her phone.

My phone vibrates between my legs. She has DMed me her post.

"Mom, I'm driving."

"Oh yeah, OK," she says, laughing. "I just posted that we're on our big journey. My followers want to know where we are and what we're doing."

"Yes they do," I say with the tone of a kindergarten teacher.

We stop for tacos in Tupelo, but don't linger. We get back in the car as soon as we've eaten. If we keep this up, we'll be in the French Quarter by dinner.

OUTSIDE NEW ORLEANS, we head to the town of Slidell. It's about twenty minutes east of the city. Mom wants to show me the house she and my dad bought right after their walk across America. It was their first home as a couple, the house where my older sister was born.

It's late afternoon, and we drive over bridges and clustered industrial areas into swampy forests and suburbia. They've built cul-de-sacs and neighborhoods in these sandy bogs. Every house seems dampened by mold at the edges. Spanish moss dangles from the trees, romantic and dirty. It looks so different from Nashville, from California. Mom is squinting her eyes at every street sign. She points at a red abandoned shack. "That was there even in 1980. It looks the same, we're getting close."

"Turn here!" she says, pointing right, giving me one second to respond. We drive down the street as she leans back in her seat. "OK, I know where we are, it's just down a ways." The houses are modest and relatively clean, with children's toys in the yards. A swing set. A fallen bike in a driveway. "There it is!" she shouts, about eight houses in on the left. It's white, two stories. It's been updated, but barely. Some paint is curling at the gutter. A sideways tricycle is in the yard. Some family lives here, with no idea that the Nissan stopped in front of their home is snapping pictures, my mom full of youth and pregnancy and young love and ambition. At least I assume she is. I am watching her hold her phone out the window. "Go slow now," she says.

"Is it weird to see this?" I ask.

"It was a good house. But we didn't want to stay in Slidell. We missed having four seasons."

"Why did you come here after the walk?"

"We met in New Orleans. It was the only place we really had in common. The place we knew. We didn't want to go where we came from, Missouri or Connecticut, you know. So we just went back. We didn't have much time to decide. I was pregnant and we had a *National Geographic* article to write."

"How do you feel right now?" I ask.

"Good," she says. I want more than that. She just keeps taking pictures.

We drive away and she puts her phone down. She's looking out the window. We don't speak. We drive into New Orleans and go to the French Quarter. "Let's just park and walk around and find somewhere to eat, unless you know somewhere you want," I say.

"Oh honey, it's been so long. I don't remember. Let's just walk around."

As we look for parking, it occurs to me that we're in a big, liberal city. They're going to have a vaccine mandate for restaurants.

My mother is not vaccinated. This is November 2021. Many cities won't let you dine indoors without proof of vaccination.

I don't know exactly why, but it infuriates me. She is seventy-four years old. Ninety percent of people over sixty-five in the United States are fully vaccinated, so it isn't even a boomer thing. It's a *my mom* thing. It's a conspiracy theory thing, I assume. I picture those radios pouring garbage into her ears all day. I picture her getting Covid, and getting hospitalized, and begging for the vaccine but it's too late, and she dies . . . and now I'm mourning and miserable *and* angry at her. I'm saying, "I told you so!" and I'm sobbing. I'm mad at her for putting me in that position.

I can't ask her about it, I can't confront her, because it's just another thing that will break my heart.

But I can be a passive-aggressive bitch. "Well, Mom, you know these restaurants are going to require proof of vaccination," I say. "I knew this would happen on our trip, we're only going to be able to eat drive-through food."

"I bet one of 'em will let us in! Let's try. It can't hurt to try!" She smiles big. We drive through the narrow streets of the French Quarter, the streets feeling more European than most anything else in America. Everything looks old. Every building has a balcony, with ornate railings. The ceilings are high, something about letting the heat rise to cool the rooms in summer. We pass a few open restaurants and I can tell we're somewhat in the center of the popular area. I park.

"Make sure you lock it," Mom says.

"I will, Mom."

"Things are different than they were. It's dangerous here now. Like many places."

"Is it?" I ask, feeling like I always have to fight her.

We begin walking. "I didn't hear it beep," she says.

"I locked it."

She walks with purpose to an ornate restaurant on the corner. There is a printed sign on the door. PROOF OF VACCINATION REQUIRED. "We can pretend we didn't see that," she chuckles. I'm annoyed.

"Hi, do you have a table for two?" she asks the host.

"It'll be about a twenty-minute wait. Can I see your vaccine card please?"

"Oh I don't have that," she says.

"I'm sorry ma'am, we can't seat you without one."

"OK!" she says, as if she's just been told she's won something. "That's fine! Have a beautiful night!"

She bops out of the restaurant. "One down, don't worry, we'll find something!"

"I'm not worried, Mom. Worry isn't the emotion."

I see a restaurant down the block, Pere Antoine, with some seating on the sidewalk. "Maybe that place will let us sit outside," I say. It is a corner building with large arched windows open to the street.

"Ooh, perfect! That looks perfect!" she says.

She floats up to the host standing in the doorway. "Do we have to be vaccinated to sit out here on these sidewalk tables?"

"Not if you're outside," he says. Or she says. Or they say. I can't tell. The host is a tall androgynous beauty. I'm always piqued when I see my mom interact with someone Fox News has told her will destroy her way of life.

"Perfect! Yay!" she exclaims, with a little clapping. "Thank you *so* much!"

We sit at a high iron table outside a big window, and she is beaming. "See, everything works out!"

"I'm concerned about the rest of our trip. I bet you need a vaccine for all of Oregon. And Colorado."

"We'll be fine! Trust!"

The streets are relatively quiet. It is a Tuesday in mid-November. The French Quarter isn't empty, but it isn't bustling.

We order chicken gumbo and gumbalaya. "What's the difference between gumbo and gumbalaya?" I ask.

"Well, jambalaya has more rice in it. So it must be their gumbo with jambalaya rice."

"I forget that New Orleans is such a part of your history."

"Absolutely it was. The French Quarter is where your dad and I had our first date. We danced and then ended the night at Café Du Monde, eating beignets."

Their first date. What a thought. My parents flirting over pastries, not knowing that they'd end up together.

My dad got the idea to walk across America after graduating college and feeling like he didn't understand his own country. It was the early seventies, the Vietnam War, an era of American discontent. He wanted to see what America was for himself. He started in upstate New York with his dog Cooper and went by foot to Washington, DC, where he convinced *National Geographic* to give him a camera to document the thing. He then walked from DC to New Orleans. The magazine took out a full-page ad in *The New York Times*. It was a photo of my father and his dog walking through Appalachia. "On October 15, 1973, Peter Jenkins took his dog out for a walk. He has yet to return."

He walked through Appalachia to middle Tennessee, where he worked on a commune farm for a few months until his dog was run over and killed. Heartbroken, he walked on to New Orleans where he stopped to write his first long article for *National Geographic*. There, he met my mother at a house party. She was in seminary, getting her master's in religious education. He pursued her for months, working on an oil rig for money while writing and chasing her. She was smitten with this chatty weirdo with an orange beard. But no matter what she felt, the relationship was red-flagged: as soon as he finished his article, he would walk the rest of the way to Oregon.

Of course she wasn't going to do that. But she was in love. My dad is an ambitious man, and he soon asked her to marry him. To marry him and walk to Oregon with him. Her instinct was *absolutely not*. She wasn't done with her master's. She wasn't the athletic type. She wasn't the sleep-in-the-dirt type. She decided she would say no. She would go to church with my dad one last time, pray for clarity from God during the service, and then break my dad's heart and say goodbye.

That morning, they got to church and sat in the front row. The pastor announced that a guest speaker would be addressing them that day. He said, "Please welcome Mom Beall." An old woman in a wheelchair rolled to the podium. My mom was intrigued. Where she came from, women couldn't speak onstage in church. Mom Beall took the mic, small and frail in her chair, and then spoke.

"Today I'm talkin' about a love story, and following God's pull on your life." Her voice was commanding, her crooked body bestowing an oracular quality on her words. "Abraham wanted his son Isaac to have a wife. He sent a servant to find him a proper wife, and the servant found a beautiful woman by a well, named Rebekah. Rebekah's family was thrilled at the idea of this union, you see. Abraham was a rich and powerful man, and Isaac was his heir. But the decision was ultimately Rebekah's."

My mother looked down at her bulletin. The title of the sermon: "Will You Go with This Man?" Her mouth went cotton dry. *Oh God, the sign.*

Needless to say, Mom Beall went on to reveal that Rebekah did go with that man. She concluded, "It's a wonder when God gets rid of stuff. It's worth everything to be free! I don't want you traveling with the pack, because God calls each of us separately."

My mom said yes. The great adventure was set in motion, and with it, a key reason I exist. Maybe somewhere deep inside she wanted to go, and she would have found a sign no matter what that sermon said. But she went. And they walked across America, starting from this city.

As we wait for our gumbo and gumbalaya, Mom says nothing about that history. She wants to book the hotel. We've decided that we'll alternate each night, so one person doesn't have to pay too much. And she wants to cover all the gas. Whenever we're together, she insists on paying for my food and anything else we buy. "I help your brother and sister out, I treat them to things, and you live all the way out in California and I can't pamper you the way I do them, so let me pay."

I am almost forty years old, and I can afford to pay for myself— for both of us, really—but something in me does love this demand. To be cared for. I am unmarried and an adult man, and I still put my mom as my emergency contact when I do anything. Most people I know put their spouse at this age. I have never done that. *Emergency Contact: Barbara Jenkins. Relation: mother.* If she lives to be ninety and I'm a solo man in this life, I'll still write her name. Expecting her to scale Mount Whitney or charter a helicopter to come rescue me from a shipwreck. Something in me will always believe she'll come find me.

While we eat, she is busy writing a post about the day. Hunched over like a fourteen-year-old girl, completely lost in her phone, giving her Instagram followers a photo dump of the day. The image makes me smile.

I post an Instagram story, a clip of her explaining the contents of our snack bag from the morning.

Her phone makes a loud jingle, a sound so loud I assume it's an Amber Alert. I post another story of us driving over a bridge into New Orleans. Another Amber Alert.

I realize she has alerts on for anything I do on Instagram. Which means every time I play drinking games with my friends, or rage against Trumpism, or post some esoteric gay meme, she gets a push notification full volume.

I'm instantly annoyed.

I mean, I know she follows me. I know she cares about what I'm doing. I know she reads my every post because she always writes a paragraph response that goes something like: *Life is full of twists and turns, but I keep my eyes pointed to Heaven. As the Bible says, "Whosoever believes shall not perish but have everlasting life."*

They all follow this format. She addresses what I've written, which is usually some critique of American Christian culture or the side effects of consumerism or death and science. Then she points it to God and quotes me a Bible verse.

Suddenly my mom springs to life from her phone. "OK, read what I've written."

"I'm eating, Mom."

"Go read it, it'll only take a moment," she says, noticing her food for the first time.

She's recapped the day.

We made it to Naw Awwlans, New Orleens, or New Orleans. Take your pick where the livin' is easy. Day 1 of our cross country road trip starts here. We will retrace the historic walk across America route that started July 4, 1976, at 3 A.M. from the city that never sleeps. A saxophone is playing in the French Quarter and people are starting to sway to the music in the streets.

"It's perfect," I say. "I hope you'll write a recap for every day of the trip!"

"Oh don't worry, I love keeping the Boomers informed. They're chomping at the bit to know how it's going and what we're seeing. They're worried we'll kill each other," she says with a laugh.

"They think that?"

"You know, not many mothers and sons can spend two weeks together," she says.

"Very true, very true. We like each other, don't we?"

"We love each other."

She pulls up HotelTonight and shows me a hotel near the airport. "This one is only $119 and looks close. Should we just book this one?"

"I'm sure it's fine," I say. "I don't care. As long as there are two beds."

"Yes, OK, I'm booking. These apps make it so easy."

We leave the restaurant and saunter through the French Quarter back to the car. We pass a group of gay men dressed in drag, with a level of outfit coordination that leads me to believe they're on a birthday trip. Red wigs, all of them. A Reba reference, perhaps.

My mom smiles at them as they pass. I wonder what she thinks. I'm sure she finds them cute. Just wouldn't want that to be her son.

We hop in the Murano and head toward the hotel.

"Oh, you know what I want? A beignet! From Café Du Monde . . . in Jackson Square I think it is."

"Aren't you so full?" I say. "I'm not really a sweets person. I never want dessert."

"I know, but we're here. I want one. I remember your dad and I getting beignets at Café Du Monde! It's gotta be close to here."

"Oh, I know where that is." It's just a couple blocks away. As I drive to it, the streets are swarming, and the spot has a line down the street. I miss my chance to park and then we're funneled to the other side of the square. "Oh shoot, wow, this might be hard to park," I say, signaling that we should give up.

"Oh shoot," she echoes looking longingly behind us. "That's OK," she says, still looking back.

"You sure? I can turn around, it just might take a minute."

"No, it's OK. I don't need the sugar," she says unconvincingly.

I put in the address of our hotel. It is close. Just eight minutes away. The French Quarter is a touristy island, and just a block or two outside its influence, you find another world. The houses become run-down. Trash in the street. The buildings shift to industrial. "Uh-oh," I say, as we seem to be entering a warehouse district. But Google insists that our hotel is just ahead. The map is confusing, roads overlapping like a knot. We wrap around a McDonald's and drive down what seems to be a utility road against the freeway, and right behind a huge industrial building is the hotel—no, wait, the industrial building *is* the hotel, and I miss the turn-in, thinking it's an alley. I U-turn and find the alley entrance. It opens up to a packed parking lot, with semi-trucks parked haphazardly on the grass out front. Large men huddle in various groups throughout the parking lot and outside of rooms, smoking cigarettes. Truckers, I assume. The lights everywhere are cold white fluorescent.

"Oh my, this is an adventure," Mom says.

We park in one of the few open spots and walk past a clump of men emitting smoke.

I grab my mom's arm. "Wow, are we going to survive this?"

"Maybe I should've looked at the photos on the website," she says, smiling, fearless.

I pull out my phone and start recording. "Mother has booked us in the shadiest hotel I've ever seen," I say to the camera. "Do you have your bong, Mother?"

"I'm gonna see if I can sell a little of it," she says.

We go to the front desk and the fluorescent lights are giving an LED flicker. The woman behind the counter is on the phone. "One second," she says and puts the phone down, not hanging up.

"Hi, we booked on HotelTonight," I say.

"Yes, OK," she says, opening a laptop that doesn't seem to be used often. She takes a credit card and we sign an agreement saying we won't smoke in the room, which feels like a losing effort. She hands us the key cards. "It's the third room down on the right, just outside on the first floor."

"Great."

We walk back outside, laughing and making eyes at each other. We feel very unified in this challenge.

We put the card in the door and open it to a burnt-smelling, simple room.

"What do you think has happened in this room before?" I say.

"Probably lots of drugs and sex and—"

"Murder?"

"Murder. Just a few things. In fact I'm praying we don't get mugged between here and the car."

I try to turn on the TV so we can watch something. A lot of hotels have smart TVs and Netflix ready to roll. The TV in this room won't turn on. Maybe the remote is dead.

I go to the front desk. As I pass the room next to ours, the door is wide open and it is clear a family lives in there. Cribs and couches and blankets and things piled to the sky. Two women stand over a third seated in a chair, doing her hair. They have colorful clothes and dark skin, black hair, and long pretty faces. They are speaking a language that I cannot understand. I see lots of kids' toys. Then I notice two children behind them. The room is so full of things, it is hard to make out the people.

I get to the lobby and ask for a new remote, because the TV doesn't work. She calls someone who seems to be the owner and puts him on speaker. He has a thick Indian accent. He tells her where the plastic bag of remotes is. She pulls one out and tells me how to program it.

I go back to the room. This remote doesn't work either. The TV doesn't do anything. There is no button on the television itself to turn it on manually.

I come back to the front desk. A woman holding a baby is in the lobby talking to the woman at the computer. They seem to know each other. "You look like you've put on weight! You look great," the woman at the computer says to the other.

I give her the remote. "The TV doesn't work and the new remote won't work either." She apologizes. I tell her we'll stream something to our laptop.

I walk back to the room. Mom has pulled a chair between the

two beds and placed her cellphone there, propped up by her pop-socket phone case. This will be our TV.

"It's important to get creative, Jed," she says. The show starts, then freezes.

"Ugggh," she grunts and picks up the phone, restarting it.

We give up and decide to just go to bed. It's 9 P.M. Plenty late to wind down. I can get lost in Instagram and TikTok for a while to get sleepy.

Mom gets out of bed and fumbles around in front of the mirror. The toilet has a door, but the sink and mirror are out in the main space. She takes out her colloidal silver, her bottle of CBD oil, and her jars of "magic oil." This is a concoction she has been working on for twenty-five years: a mix of a dozen different oils, hyaluronic acid, onion extract, and only God and Barb know what else. It's the color of melted butter, and she smears it on her face every morning and every night. At home, I have seen her come out of her "layer" (bedroom) with a shiny face and no makeup, getting water from the kitchen before going to sleep. That is a normal occurrence, but it is intriguing to see her get ready for bed in front of me. The removing of makeup. Washing the face. Taking vitamins. I don't know what to make of it, but it feels consequential, to see her like this.

She turns off the light by the sink, shuffles over to bed, and grunts as she gets under the covers. Then she scoots her weight to get comfortable, props a pillow so she can sit up, puts on headphones, and starts swiping through her phone. I wonder what she's looking at.

She giggles. She is holding the screen close to her face. Her face is dewy and shimmering. Her tittering won't stop.

"Mom!" I say. She can't hear me. I wave my hands to get her attention.

She takes one headphone out of her ear. "What?"

"What are you watching?"

"Ooh, baby elephants. I search 'baby elephants' on YouTube and watch for hours."

"Like, regularly?"

"Every night."

She smiles. "Oh," she says, remembering something, "let me read us a devotion from my little book. It's called *Power Prayers: Warfare That Works* and it's prayers for specific things. There's one in there for road trips!"

"OK," I say, acquiescing.

She pulls a little book from her bag. It has the worst-designed cover I've ever seen. Of course it does. The words *Power* and *Prayers* are set in giant type across the top, exploding out of a cloud that shoots lightning bolts in every direction. It looks like a Power-Point slide from 1997. Why do fundamentalist faith and artistic skill rarely coexist?

"OK, lemme see," she says, flipping through. "Here we go." She sits up and shifts her weight, playfully. "Father, in the name of Jesus, I thank you that you have given me dominion now. I exercise that dominion now over the fowl of the air and everything that creeps on the earth, and I command them to stay out of my roadway—in other words, not to hit a deer," she says as an aside.

"This is so specific."

"Mmm . . . I speak supernatural, mechanical, and physical preservation over this automobile. I speak supernatural gas mileage and supernatural travel time. Lord, if possible, I ask that you would translate me to my destination. I don't really know what all that means," she says with a chuckle. "I bind every rock and loose article on the road, and every spirit that causes accidents, in Jesus'

name. I bind and break the power of curses placed on the road-
ways. And bind every bloodthirsty spirit that hovers over the
highways. And I bind all spirits of harassment from city policemen and highway patrolmen, and I command you to be occupied
when I pass through your city. In the name of Jesus." As she reads,
she looks over at me to make sure the words land with a punch.
"While I am away, I appoint mighty angels to stand guard around
my property shoulder to shoulder, that no evil penetrate. And I
thank you for a safe trip to and from."

"That is strange," I say, laughing. "Why are we binding police
officers?"

"We're not binding them, we're just . . ."

"Why are we binding rocks to the road, God doesn't care."

"Well—"

"He wants us to be safe I guess—"

"Of course he does."

"—unless he doesn't."

"But the enemy of our souls doesn't. He seeks to steal, kill, and
destroy. So, basically, we're praying just as Jesus said, 'Deliver us
from evil' in the Lord's Prayer. This is basically a specific prayer of
delivering us from accidents, from . . . I mean, there are policemen
and highway patrolmen that just look for somebody to stop. So it's
just protection as we travel."

"Well that's great, loved it," I say.

"OK great." She puts her headphones back in, turns off the
lamp, and settles back into the baby elephants.

I'm lying on my back, and the room is flickering in the light of
her iPhone screen. The air conditioner is loud and rattling. Even
though it is fall and chilly, I like having it on for the noise. My
mom's prayer has comforted me. Binding cops and roadkill. I'm

smiling in bed. To believe that every step is being watched over, planned by the Most High. Then I picture the baby elephants. My mother grinning into her phone. Clicking through a YouTube rabbit hole of cute trunks and ears. That isn't something a "mother" does, but a person. A girl on her phone in bed.

A thought I'm trying to jam into my understanding: a mother is just a person. A teenage girl who got older. A human who got pregnant and raised kids the best she could. I know my mom, in her early thirties, saw the rosy projection of her life on the wall before her. Growing old with her rugged, famous husband. Kids on the way. A farmhouse in the countryside. More books. More magazine covers. A big Christian ministry, perhaps.

Just like I, in my thirties, imagine all the wonderful things to come for me.

The erosion of dreams seems to be a feature of aging. When you're young, you think, *Maybe I'm good at Ping-Pong, or graphic design; I've never tried. Maybe my future husband is a doctor, or a firefighter. I haven't met him yet. Maybe I'll be famous. Maybe I'll be a teacher. I haven't opened many doors, but what if the best, loveliest thing is behind the next one? There's a chance, right?*

So many of my mother's dreams pulled away from her. Her daughter was a rebel, sneaking out at night and coming home high. I would fall asleep to the sounds of their shouting in the kitchen, punctuated by a slap across a cheek. The middle child (me) was effeminate. When I was two, my dad wondered aloud, "Maybe he's gay." My mom was incensed. "How could you say such a thing about your own child?" The third, another son, had major health problems from the jump. Mom said she thought it was from the stress of discovering my dad's escapades during the pregnancy.

Then the divorce. Her marriage, once a beacon to the community and Christians around the country, became a cautionary tale. Newspapers printed stories of my father's infidelity, of a battle for custody. The good Christian fans turned. The interviews dried up. The book deals withered. She cut coupons and took us camping at Big South Fork State Park because it was the only vacation she could afford. She was always picking up my sister from the police station or taking my brother to doctor after doctor. I never saw her watching TV or drinking wine on the couch. I never saw her rest. She remarried when I was nine, and that man left her four years later for the secretary. After that, I noticed that she did not bring a man over for dinner, or even go on dates as far as I could tell. Occasionally she would mention a man from church. "He is nice. I'm not attracted to him, but he is nice to me."

The lovely possibilities of the future had faded. Reality took the house she'd imagined brick by brick.

My mother clicks the phone dark and sets it beside her under the covers and rolls onto her side, away from me. She has not taken her headphones out. She falls asleep to something. Music? A podcast? What is she thinking about? I picture her alone in her big house, surrounding herself with the sound of elephants trumpeting and voices of doom.

3

. . .

WE SURVIVE THE NIGHT in the hotel, but I wake up in pain. There is a stabbing sensation in my neck, like one of the tendons is angry and burning. But the real killer is in my upper abdomen. This feels like a barbed spear is in my side, and being twisted with an evil grin.

This pain started when I was in Europe the previous August for a friend's birthday. I tried wakeboarding when we were out in the Mediterranean one day. My friends, most of whom are in their late thirties—the same age as me—took turns sitting in that water holding on to that rope. The boat would roar to full speed, and each of them would stand up on the little board with a smile. Easy as can be. That gave me confidence. They told me it's intuitive. You just push on the water with your feet, stand up, and glide over the wake like a sexy angel.

Well, I tried this. I sat, ass in the water, feet on the board, hands holding the triangle grip, as the driver friend in his blue Oakley sunglasses yelled back, "READY?"

"READY!" I screamed, chancing a thumbs-up and snapping my hand back to the rope.

The boat lurched forward, the coiled rope quickly pulling taut, and POW, I was yanked to hell. The rope was gone, out of my hands.

OK, OK, I can do this, I thought. Hold on *tighter*. Which seemed impossible. But my friends, my female friends with their small delicate wrists, had been standing up all afternoon. What was my problem?

I tried again. I was gripping the rope with my whole body and flinching and basically trying to hold the boat back. It ripped me forward and waterboarded me for a couple of seconds and I let go again.

The boat circled around and I gripped the handle for the third time. I turned green like the Hulk with rage and commitment. *I will. Stand. Up.* The rope jerked and vanished from my hand again. *Fuck this*.

I pitifully doggy-paddled back to the boat and could tell I was about to be sore in places I didn't know I had muscles. For the rest of the afternoon, my friends glided on the wakes and lovingly reminded me that it's very hard to get the hang of.

We were all staying at a house on a cliff above the water. One friend revealed that he had procured molly and we were going to have a big night. Make drinks. Play in the pool. Blast music. And bliss out with some serotonin overdose.

We decided to have a light dinner to make the experience . . . brighter. We made ourselves drinks. The pills were paraded out on a serving tray. "Would you like to swallow it straight or mix it with water?" I decided to empty my pill into a water bottle. It's a slower release. Sometimes the rush of a swallowed pill can be too much.

I sip. You sip. We sip. Life was grand. We were jumping in the pool. Aperol spritzes were made. It feels more like a daytime drink, but we were on vacation and celebrating and doing what we wanted, when we wanted. We sat on the patio. The furniture and the conversation were lush. I reminisced about my wakeboarding failure. We raved about the temperature and clarity of the Mediterranean Sea. About thirty minutes in, the glow began. My body was warm and happy. I found myself listening to my friends with a smile ear to ear, just happy they exist and that we exist together on earth at the same time. A few friends jumped into the pool. We switched to dance music. "PLAY ROBYN!" someone shouted. We were chain-smoking. Molly makes a cigarette seem not only healthy but necessary.

About an hour into this experience, something tightened inside me. Not metaphorically, not emotionally. Literally. Something in my body was seizing. It felt like a muscle spasm. In my upper abdomen. Let's pretend I have a six-pack: the top right ab was cramping like a contraction. Like a charley horse. I raised my arms to try to stretch it out. I lay on the ground and put my arms above my head, which at the moment seemed like the only way to escape being sucked into the black hole of my ab.

"What are you doing?" my friend asked, smiling at the absurdity of me writhing on the floor.

"I have incredible pain in my ab, it's crazy!" I said this like I was telling a funny story. She laughed.

"Why are you so happy? Are you serious?" She was delighted. I was too.

"I don't know, but the pain is at a ten!" I cackled.

The juxtaposition of pain and molly was a new experience. My brain was in full bliss mode, but I was still me and I was rational, and I could think clearly. Molly simply tells your brain that everything is beautiful or at least cute.

I continued to wiggle and stretch to try to pull the cramp out from my ribs. I wiggled and bent my body for about an hour and the spasm ended. My friends were overjoyed that I'd lived. We all jumped into the pool and the party went on.

A few days later, the pain returned when I was flying back to the US. Not as intense as the night of the party, but the knot in my abdomen was there. I wasn't flying home, but straight to Colorado to meet my mom and Glenda for a road trip around the Rockies.

When I landed in Denver, the pain was still a dull, strange thing. My mom and Glenda picked me up and we headed to a hotel. The next day we were driving to the top of a mountain, and up there something shifted. The pain was so intense I could hardly drive. It was coming every three or four minutes, in spasms like dagger strikes. The neck pain, the shooting tendon, they were happening in tandem and it was worse than ever.

I texted Toby, a friend who's an ER doctor in San Francisco. I explained the stabbing pain. Could it be some knot in my intestines, or a blood clot? It felt like something is in there trying to burst. He writes me back immediately. "The only thing I don't want it to be is a pulmonary embolism. A blood clot from the leg that moves up to the heart. You're young for that but you did just fly on a ten-hour flight and that's when it can happen."

When I googled this, I read that it happens to men over forty, a blood clot in the shin that moves up through the veins and can get stuck in the lung. It can be fatal. One-third of people with untreated pulmonary embolisms die. My eyes widened and my brain tingled with adrenaline. My peripheral vision turned to static. *Am I going to pass out?* I thought.

I noticed the location of my current pain, exactly where a lung is. I thought about flying to Europe. Ten hours there. I thought about flying back. Ten more hours. I am a window-seat guy, and I can stay there the whole flight. Which I did.

Sitting at a café in Colorado with my mom and Glenda across from me, I turned ghostly gray. I was reading the WebMD to them. Glenda said we should find a clinic and get it checked out now. Toby texted saying that the best way to get a proper check is to go to the ER. I'd need a CT scan and an ultrasound.

I found the closest ER on Google. Mom could see that I was drained of blood and had terror in my eyes. "Let me drive us, honey," she said, calm as can be. I moved to the backseat and sat, spinning out with worry. *A blood clot is trying to kill me, I'm too young, it's the cigarettes, I'm fucked.*

"Let's say a prayer for healing," my mom suggested.

"Lord Jesus, we ask for your healing and mercy on Jed, we ask that you take away any pain and any blood clots or problems, we plead the blood of Jesus on this situation and we know you are in control, and you are good and have all good things for those that follow you, we ask that Jed will trust you more and more with his life and that you'll show yourself and take this pain away and give him a clean bill of health. We plead your name over the doctor and that we'll get into the hospital fast with no waiting, and that everything will be perfectly fine, in Jesus' name we pray, amen."

Mom drove toward the hospital with one knee as she fished in her purse. "Let me find my bong!"

She found her nebulizer and turned it on. Vapor started pumping out. She took a big inhale, one pull on each nostril. "OK let's get some colloidal silver in those lungs, to heal you in Jesus' name, I pray!"

I was scared enough to inhale the nonsense.

At the ER, Glenda waited in the car while Mom and I went in. I had hardly ever been to the hospital in my life, and I was grateful to have my mom beside me. She was not frazzled by this change of plans. She didn't seem to think a visit to the ER is odd at all. Like it was bound to happen. She was chipper and thought my worry was cute.

We checked in and I described my pain and we waited for only a few minutes. "Can my mom come back with me?" I asked.

"Of course," the nurse said. I wonder if my voice was higher, smaller, more pitiful. I'm thirty-eight years old and my mom was walking me back to the doctor's office.

They ran test after test. At one point, the doctor dug his hands under my rib cage and I yelped in pain. Not from some injury he discovered but from the depth of his poke. He said he was feeling to see if my gallbladder is inflamed. The EKG machine rolled in and they covered me with sticky sensors and cords. My mom was playing a word game on her phone.

They did an ultrasound. They did an X-ray. I was glad they were doing so much and I was wondering how much this would cost. I have the cheapest insurance possible. My deductible is $7,000, and this hospital was out of network. *My God*. But I was so worried about this blood clot in my guts, I was willing to pay my last dollar to know what was wrong.

They left me and Mom in the room for a while. I filmed an Instagram story describing my situation. "Update from the ER, I'm getting probed and I don't hate it." I tried to stay positive and laugh. To channel my mom's cool. I sent friends selfies from the hospital bed.

The doctor returned holding his chart. He sat down next to me.

"You know, we can't find a single thing wrong with you. Every test is coming back clear. I think what we've got here is . . . a pulled muscle. The upper abdominals, right at the rib cage."

I thought of the wakeboarding mishap. Me using my whole body to fight a speedboat. I thought of the molly spasm the night after.

"You're all clear. Abdominal muscles take a long time to heal, and you don't have anything to worry about. Just don't be doing any sit-ups," the doctor said.

I was relieved. It might cost me several thousand dollars, but at least I knew I didn't have a deadly blood clot. I thanked the doctor and my mom was smiling and calm and not surprised.

As we walked out, she put her hand on my shoulder.

"Prayer works, Jed. Just a pulled muscle."

Soon after, the pain left. We finished that road trip, and I went back to California thinking the ab must have healed.

But now, here I am in New Orleans, without having done one sit-up or side bend, and the pain is back, as bad as ever.

I text Toby the doctor again.

"OK, new interesting update. Remember my potential pulmonary embolism that turned out to be a pulled muscle in my rib . . . Well it's back, from doing nothing. And it's most pronounced in that same spot near the gallbladder, but it's also uncomfortable all over my guts. As if my intestines are mad. Makes me wonder if I have developed a gnarly allergy to something I regularly eat? Just keeping you updated . . ."

"Hey," he replies. "How long has this been going on this time?

Have you tried anything that makes it better (tried any meds?)? Any obvious changes with certain foods (any foods that seem to make it worse?)? Any focal areas of tenderness in your belly? Is all the pain localized to the right upper belly?"

I tell him I'm traveling and driving all day, but no real diet changes.

He doesn't write me back. He's an ER doctor after all. Probably sewing someone together. I decide I'll watch what I eat. Maybe I've developed a food allergy.

I get up gingerly out of bed. My hand is on my abs, I'm walking with a hunch, hobbling to the curtains to let some morning light in. Mom opens her eyes. "Good morning honey, is it time to go?"

"Let's get this trip down memory lane on the road," I say with a wince, but trying to sound bright.

She throws off the covers and swings her legs over the side of the bed. She rubs her eyes, yawns. "Let me put my face on," she says.

We PACK UP and wave goodbye to the crusty hotel. There's a McDonald's next door, so I down a Sausage McMuffin with egg. Mom forces her hash browns on me.

"I'm certain this hotel is close to the church your dad and I got married in. I don't know exactly where it is, but it was called Word of Faith Temple. Let's drive by it first."

I search for it on Google Maps in the area just east of New Orleans, and the church pops up. It's only half a mile away.

We drive past strip malls and Pep Boys and more McDonald's. And there it is. A brick church surrounded by power lines and boxy commercial buildings. Not big, not small. A building that would catch no one's eye.

"They haven't updated it," Mom says, taking a photo with her phone. "Looks just the same."

"How big was your wedding?"

"About 150," she says.

I wonder who those 150 people were. Family, of course. But that would amount to maybe thirty. Who are all those other people? Where are they now?

It feels wrong that this would be the church. This place, holy in the story of me, so boring and invisible to every car that drives by it. Life feels random and meaningless to me in a flash. Shouldn't the moments in history shine? Grand, like a cathedral?

Then I soften, realizing that every ugly brick structure in the world is someone's most important fork in the road. Mom looks out the window, her face blank but warm. One hundred fifty guests who came from all over to celebrate her love. The beginning of happily ever after. I wonder what she feels. I assume it hurts, to see this place of hope and joy that ended in collapse. Or maybe she is nostalgic for the purity of that day.

I don't press her to say how she feels. We drive on and the thick moment is gone.

"OK, where to next?" I say, moving past history like we're running errands.

"My seminary," she says. "Plug in New Orleans Baptist Theological Seminary." I do. This is the place where my mom studied for her master's degree in Christian education. She was the first of her family to go to college, and then the first to pursue a graduate degree. By the time she enrolled, she was almost thirty. An unmarried Christian woman from the Ozarks. In the 1970s, this was considered geriatric, a failure, or madness. Why would she be studying instead of urgently locking in a man?

We drive ten minutes into the suburbs just northeast of New Orleans. The houses are big and old and many are run down, evidence of a rich neighborhood past its prime. We arrive at a campus of brick buildings, some resembling old Southern mansions, others looking like midcentury boxy dorms. The only zhuzh being white shutters on the plain rectangular structures.

"This is where I studied, getting my master's, this is where I met your dad," she says as we pull into a large parking lot for what seems to be an auditorium. "This building is new." Her voice sounds distant as she examines the place. She's deep in her head, rummaging through files and folders, pulling old photos and feelings out of the vault.

We park next to that auditorium and walk through the parking lot toward the rest of the campus. There are more brick buildings, all built around a church with a tall steeple. A black wrought-iron fence wraps the perimeter. It is November and the whole place feels abandoned. Maybe because it's 8 A.M. Even this late in the year, it's 75 degrees. I cannot imagine rushing across this campus in July.

We walk like she's following a smell. "I had class in this building, and I lived right over here," she says.

"So, how'd you meet Dad? Why was he here?"

"One of my friends was having a party in her dorm, and someone invited him. He was staying with a professor. He showed up and he was different from everyone else. Long hair. Bearded. Looking like a hippie. The party turned into a water fight. Someone threw their water on someone else to be funny and it became a war. He was standing in the door when I flung it open and I threw water on him. Here in this dorm, here. That's how I met Peter Jenkins."

"Wow," I say, imagining my parents young and strangers to each other.

"Your dad and I collected walnuts from the grove here," she says, pointing to a group of trees that don't look like walnut.

"Are you sure? These don't look like walnut trees to me."

"Well I can't remember," she says. "I thought it was here." As we walk, a young man passes us. He makes the mistake of saying, "Good morning."

"Good morning," Mom says. "I went here in 1975!"

"Oh really?" He stops walking, with pulling-away body language that says *don't trap me.*

"Yes. I went here in 1975 and I met his father—this is my son, Jed—and his father and I left from right here on this campus and we walked to Oregon."

"Really? Walked?" He shifts his weight and plants his feet. He's realized he'll be here for a while.

"Oh yes. And my son here and I are driving to Oregon, retracing our steps," she says, beaming.

"That is awesome. Well, good luck to you." He seems genuinely happy for us.

I cringe when my mother forces strangers into conversations with her friendliness, but then I see this man, lifted from his moment with her.

"Isn't this just a gorgeous day!" she says to him.

"Yes it is," he says, looking up and realizing that she is right.

"Are you a student here?"

"No, I'm a professor."

"Oh wow, you look so young! Well, that's because I'm an old lady, everyone looks young."

"You aren't old! You're beautiful," he says.

OK, I've had enough of this Southern love-bombing.

"It was nice to meet you," I say through a smile, then I turn to her. "Mom, come on. We have a long drive ahead of us."

The man nods, "You two have a great day."

"We surely will!" Mom says. "Now this is where the president of the college lived. Right here on campus," she waves her hand palm up to a two-story brick house with columns.

On the walk back to the car, she's smiling to herself. We get in and pull onto the road that runs along the front of campus toward downtown New Orleans. "This is where we started," she says, pointing to the sidewalk. "We walked right here." The road is unremarkable. Just next to campus is a run-down theater with boarded-up windows. I would've pictured them starting the walk at City Hall, or at the Gulf of Mexico, or some iconic arch or statue. No. They just walked out the gates of the campus and pointed themselves to Oregon.

Driving toward downtown New Orleans and the long bridges that reach west, I cannot see how they walked through this. It is no bucolic country road. It is industrial grime, gray and cracked.

"We left on the Fourth of July at 3 A.M. It was unbearably hot."

"Why on earth would you leave in the middle of summer??"

"Because it was 1976, the two-hundredth birthday of America. It felt like an important day to start." I never knew or connected that they left on this day. I have also never read their books, the ones that made my parents famous. I'm not sure why. They littered our houses. My mom had two shelves full of them. My dad had a room dedicated to them. They are required reading in lots of high schools across America.

For the longest time, I wasn't exactly interested in their lives.

"Here, let me read to you about it," she says, and pulls out her copy of *The Walk West*. She flips and finds the page. It is clotted with bookmarks and tagged pages. She has prepared for this show-and-tell.

"We had chosen 3 A.M., just three hours after the Fourth. We'd be able to slip out of the city under the cover of the jungle-warm darkness. It seemed appropriate for this part of the country. We chose 3 A.M. because we could take an anniversary stroll through the French Quarter. After all, our first walk through the French Quarter kicked off this whole thing between us. We'd let the gas lanterns flicker on us one last time." She closes the book and takes off her reading glasses and looks out onto the road.

We pull into a McDonald's for some breakfast. As we wait in the line, there is a young man holding a sign. "Any Help Appreciated."

"He looks healthy, what a shame," my mom says. "I'll give him a dollar. Should I tell him—"

"No Mom," I say. I don't even know what she wanted to say. The gospel? To get a job? It doesn't matter. I tell her she shouldn't say a word. She rolls down her window and hands him a few dollars. "Here you go, sweety. God bless you." He nods furiously with gratitude and doesn't make a sound. He seems to be mute.

I think about the dollars my mother just gave this man. I never give homeless people money. Mostly because I was at a conference once and heard the head of the LA Mission say that we shouldn't. He said that the city has all the services the homeless could need—plenty of food, et cetera—and if you give a homeless person a dollar, you "rent his spot on the sidewalk for another day." I also never have cash on me. Well, that's not true. I usually have a twenty. But I'm not giving a homeless person twenty dollars unless I'm overcome with altruism. Which I never am. I don't know why. Maybe the complexity of homelessness paralyzes me. Should I be helping upstream, donating to homeless organizations instead of homeless people directly? Picketing for affordable housing in my city? Slashing landlords' tires? It feels too big for me. I think about my good liberal values, my analytical mind, my *New York Times* subscription . . . and I think about my mom handing that man two dollars. And the likelihood that she will pray for him tonight.

He keeps waving at my mom as she rolls up the window, smiling wide. If I had been alone, the most he would've gotten would have been a cautious grin of acknowledgment and my averted eyes.

We drive west out of New Orleans and the industrial scene gives way to long, low bridges running over swamps. The land and water seem to be in constant conversation, with globs of plants rising out of mud and water. My mom is staring down into the muck. "We must've camped right in there the first night," she says.

"In where? The swamp??"

"Oh yes. The bugs were terrible. The mosquitoes."

"Are there alligators?"

"Of course."

What a hellish way to begin a cross-country walk.

"How did you sleep? How did you feel starting the walk like this?"

"Horribly. I remember we were being followed by a suspicious car, so at one point, right around here, we jumped off the road into a soggy grove of these tall pines and dead trees. We stood still, waiting for the car to lose us, and then we found a flat place and pitched our tent. I was so scared and uncomfortable. I remember before I fell asleep I heard a splash in the bayou and I could've sworn I heard footsteps. I barely slept that night."

"Who was following you? Did you have a stalker?"

"No idea. I just remember being terrified and thinking I'd made the biggest mistake of my life."

We review her trip binder and see that the route bends down near the coast, though not the kind of coast you might picture. Being the mouth of the Mississippi River, it is a hundred square miles of marshy islands and mangroves. It's less sandy beach than a shape-shifting mess of muck.

As we drive, I see a destroyed house, then one without a roof, then piles of shredded walls and aluminum siding in people's yards. "What happened here, I wonder?" I ask.

"Looks like a hurricane. I think this must be Ida," Mom says. I've never seen hurricane damage up close. We drive for miles and miles and every house has a mountain of rubbish piled at the front of the yard. This looks like weeks of cleanup, and it is still a wasteland. I see people walking through minced houses, picking up boards and shingles and tossing them onto this pile or that.

Between small towns are fields of what looks like giant grass. "That's sugarcane," Mom says. I see trucks piled high with harvested stalks, headed to big facilities that pump thick clouds of white smoke into the air. The smoke seems like pollution, but Google reveals that it is steam. The sugarcane is crushed in giant rollers to separate the juice from the fiber, and then the fiber is boiled. I had no idea Louisiana grew so much sugar.

We cross through Lafayette and Lake Charles and arrive just beyond the border of Texas in Jasper. I've never been to this part of Texas and it doesn't feel like Texas. I mean the people do. So do the trucks and hats and the HELL IS REAL billboards. But the land is still Louisiana to me. I'm intrigued by all the pine trees. I associate pine trees with the mountains, not the hot South, but my association is wrongly small. They grow here by the billions.

"Let me read you some more from this stretch," she says, pulling out her book again. "I'll read you the part where we came upon this amazing violinist on the side of the road." She flips pages and finds it.

"Tell me stranger, are you walking across country just to see if you can do it or are you getting to know the folks?"

"We're walking so that we can meet people that we'd never meet otherwise. Walking makes us open up to them and them to us." He placed his violin case on the road. He carefully reached out his hand and offered it to me. "I don't know your name brother but what you and she are doin' is something I can relate to." We shook hands. He was a street musician unlike anyone I'd ever seen anywhere.

She closes the book. "See, we met so many amazing, interesting people."

The sun gets three-quarters through the sky and it's time to look for a hotel. This time I book the room. A Holiday Inn Express. Easy and dependable. It also has a gym. I want to try to get a workout in if I'm going to be sitting in a car for eight to nine hours a day. My pain is rising, coming back. Per usual, I hadn't noticed its absence all day. I never notice when I'm healthy. But now it's returning like a tide. The combination of the neck, the abdominal pain, the twisting stabbing . . . It can't be my pulled abdominal anymore. That shit would heal. What on earth? Maybe the doctor in Colorado was wrong. Maybe the pulled muscle was a distraction, a ruse, for a real serious problem. A real blood clot or something. Stories of misdiagnoses, malpractice lawsuits, and arrogant doctors missing obvious clues ping-pong in my head.

As we drive into east Texas, the pine trees tall and the land rising in small hills, I hold my hand across my belly, the pain raging. It really hurts this time, maybe worse than before.

We find our hotel just off the highway. The Holiday Inn Express looks like all the others, a silver-paneled refrigerator laid on its side. The structure is crisp like a computer rendering, clean and fake. Mom sees my hand clutching my gut and is watching me with a furrowed brow. "Oh honey, does it hurt?"

"So bad."

I am hurried as we check in. I need to lie down, to change my position or stretch and contort to figure out a way for it to hurt less. I have to stand—rib cage up and shoulders pulled back—so as not to cause a painful spasm. I barely acknowledge the human behind the counter, and we head upstairs to the room. Mom sits on the bed and starts to google. She's on WebMD. Here we go.

"It sounds like an ulcer. You just have an ulcer. No, a hernia. It could be a hernia or an ulcer."

"I read all that, I don't think it's that."

"Or a food allergy!"

I'm somewhat convinced it could be an allergic reaction to something I'm eating. Maybe my body is rejecting lactose? Gluten? Eggs? Red meat? What can I cut out to make this stop?

I decide I'm not going to drink alcohol or eat any cheese or bread for this road trip. Maybe that'll do something. Also it might be nice to take a break from those things. A side-skinny hustle in the name of ending this horrific pain. Something in me hopes it works, so I am forced to eat healthy forever.

I don't text Toby because I always text him when I'm sick. Instead I text my friend's brother who's also a doctor. I describe my symptoms and apologize for bothering him. He calls me. Which scares me. I step into the hall. On the phone he's calm and just wants to ask me more questions. I tell him about the stabbing pain. I tell him about my ER visit months ago. The "pulled muscle." How it can't be that anymore. Maybe it's my gallbladder? An inflamed intestine? I just word vomit. When I'm done talking, he says, "Everything you've described sounds exactly like a pulled abdominal muscle. Those muscles take a long time to heal. They're used almost all the time, so they don't get to rest. You just need to make sure you treat it gently and don't exercise it. And while you're at it, eat bland food, just to make sure it isn't something else or acid reflux. Don't eat anything spicy."

His calmness makes me feel much better. The pain is still stabbing, but now that I have reasonable assurance that it isn't me dying, I am relieved.

As we get ready for bed, the TV plays the local news quietly and Mom is watching her YouTube videos on her phone. I turn on the air conditioner.

"Oh no, not that again. It's already so cold," she says.

"I love the cold and I need the white noise!"

"Fine. I'll just freeze to death," she says, smiling.

"You'll be fine."

"Let me just pull this cardboard blanket over me," she adds, which makes me laugh. Laughing sends me into a horrific spasm of pain.

"Ow, ow, ow, ow Mom, don't be funny!" It feels like I'm being filleted.

This, unfortunately, gives my mom the church giggles.

"This paper will keep me warm," she says under her breath, clutching her bad Holiday Inn blanket and holding in a giggle, which makes her shake.

"OW. OW. OWWW!"

She's laughing harder now, this demon woman. I'm laughing too. I have to climb out of bed and go out into the bathroom to get away from her and make the spasms stop.

Finally, finally, with controlled breathing like I'm in labor, the contractions end. My insides have been ripped to shreds. The muscle feels like it's torn away from my stomach, aching and sharp and wounded. But the spasms have stopped.

I carefully walk back into the room and breathe slowly.

"Mom you almost killed me!"

"I caught the church laughs. I couldn't stop, I'm so sorry!"

I crawl into bed gently.

"I'm gonna pray for you," she says. "I'm going to lay hands on you." She hops out of bed, goes to her bag, and digs through it until she's holding up a little bottle of anointing oil.

As she sits on the edge of my bed, I am teleported to childhood. Every night she sat on the side of my bed to say a goodnight prayer. I couldn't sleep until this ritual was completed. I don't know the last time I did my goodnight prayers. The last time happened, and I didn't notice. But I'm noticing now. We haven't done this ritual in thirty years.

She somehow manifests a cup of colloidal silver out of thin air. And then a bottle of pills called Texas SuperFood. "Drink this and swallow these," she says. I obey. Then she takes the anointing oil and puts some on her hand. "This is frankincense." She dots it on my forehead. Then she puts her hand on my stomach and begins to pray. "God, we ask you to take this pain away, we bind any spirits of pain. We bind any food allergies. We bind any ulcers . . ."

Her eyes are closed and her hand is warm and soft on my stomach. My eyes are open, looking at her hand. I can't stop looking at it. I imagine some magic flowing into me. The five-year-old boy beneath my skin, who I forgot was in there, feels cradled.

"We ask for miraculous healing in the name of Jesus," she finishes. "Amen."

She opens her eyes and flashes a grin, jolting back from reverent ceremony to childlike lightness. "That wasn't so bad was it? OK, I bet your pain will be gone in the morning."

Then she puts away her potions and crawls back into bed.

THE NEXT MORNING I wake up and my pain is less, but still there. I pull the blinds and Mom gets out of bed and starts collecting her things. I go down to the lobby and get a coffee, a hard-boiled egg, and a green banana. I come back up and the coffee has started doing its work. I need the bathroom.

I have a seat on the toilet and hear rustling around in the room. Then the room door opens and, just before it closes, I hear her gasp out in the hall. A yelp of "No!" I immediately know she has locked herself out. She went out there for God knows what and forgot a key.

I'm on the toilet. I can't exactly hop up. I roll my eyes.

I wait for her to text me. Or bang on the door or yell my name. No sound. Silence. I bet she doesn't have her phone. She's going to start banging. I'm going to have to shout from this toilet that she'll just have to wait. She doesn't bang.

I finish and leave the bathroom and open the door to the hall. She's standing right there. In silence. Her head lowered. A small, ashamed smile. She didn't knock. She just waited, knowing I would be annoyed. *What a goose.* I know she hates feeling dumb, so I just shake my head and let her back in. I don't smile or laugh to ease the moment. I wish I had. But I didn't.

We get back in the car and head west. Today our goal is Amarillo or near there. It takes a full day of driving just to cross Texas.

As we pass through towns with small hills and more pine trees, I look at the houses. Victorians built by doctors and lawyers in the 1900s. Bungalows built in the 1920s and '30s. Ranch houses from the 1950s and '60s. Whenever we're stopped, I open Zillow and set my location to whatever east Texas town I'm in. Some of these houses are $200,000. They're beautiful. The big ones go for $500,000. I think of how expensive Los Angeles is. How pricey Nashville is getting. If you're willing to live anywhere, you can find a beautiful house for a modest amount of money. The problem is: How do you make money? Where do you find culture? Where do you find friends?

The towns recede and farms emerge and new towns arrive. I picture my parents walking every mile. "Read me a little more from the book," I say.

"Sure, lemme find something from this stretch." She searches for a minute and lifts the book up to read. "This was right after your dad and I got in a huge fight."

We'd cooled down our tempers by this time but I was still the filthiest I'd ever been. I longed for a cool leisurely bath in an air-conditioned room. I was crusty with dirt and my face was streaked from the tears this morning. I was desperate for a bath. Most laundromats had public bathrooms but this one only had a stool. No sink and no running water where I could at least splash cold water on my face. The longer I sat in that hot laundromat in my own sweat and stench the more desperate I became. I knew what I would do. I grabbed my handkerchief and locked the bathroom door behind me. I flushed the stained toilet bowl five times and could see the water was as clean as it would get. I dipped my cloth into the bowl and soaked it down. I squeezed the cool water down my legs and arms, flushing the toilet over and over to keep the water clean. Then I scooped up a handful and washed my face. My bar of Ivory soap covered up the smell of urine that penetrated the dirty room.

"Wow, Mom, that sounds horrible. You're so tough."

"I really wasn't. I was very feminine, but the road forces you to be strong."

We stop for gas at a big station, one with a built-in McDonald's and nice bathrooms. There are camouflage hats that say "Let's Go Brandon" on them, and statues of horses and cowboys on the shelves. Mom gets a monstrous Styrofoam cup and starts filling it with half sweet tea and half unsweetened tea. "Looks good," a man behind her says. He is tall, maybe sixty-five years old or so, and has an accent. Eastern Europe, perhaps. The sounds of a heavy tongue and a Bond villain. "You like tea?" he asks. I know flirting when I see it. This large man is flirting with my mom.

"Oh yes, I love tea. Unsweet tea, but then with a splash of sweet." Her voice is sunny like a young girl's.

"A splash of sweet, like you," he says.

"Oh!" she laughs. "I am sweet, aren't I."

She finishes filling her tea and goes down an aisle to see if she wants anything crunchy for the car. The big man follows her. He shadows her, pretending he's shopping, but wanting to keep an eye on her. This sounds creepy as I write it, but I assure you it wasn't. It was cute.

We get back in the car, and Mom is sipping her tea, smiling, looking straight ahead.

"Mom, that man was obsessed with you."

"Oh hush. No he wasn't."

"He was flirting with you! He saw you and couldn't handle himself. He was following you around the gas station."

"He was? Well . . ."

We say nothing more about it. I pull the car from the gas station and I can feel her glowing beside me, her mind turning over with nice feelings.

We make it to the town of Athens for lunch. The landscape has changed from forested hills to big open ranches. Not entirely flat, but more a crumpled duvet. There are McDonald's and Wendy's and various chains, but I want to find a local place. Something that exists only in this little town. I find a Mexican diner. Sounds promising.

We pull in and there are lots of cars. Also promising.

Inside are vinyl wood-print walls and booths with red benches. Perfect. A small lady with a Mexican accent tells us we can sit wherever we like. It's lunchtime and most of the place is full. We find a table near the back.

At one table there are four young guys in their twenties. They wear camo hats and thick T-shirts that look to be made of cardboard. Their facial hair is sparse and unkempt, a little too long. But they all look alike, so apparently it's just right in their eyes. They are laughing together, and I wonder what their life is.

At another table is an old couple, a man and wife. They are wrinkled and overweight and the woman's white hair is long, pulled back into a ponytail. Their hands are folded in front of them, their eyes are closed, and they are praying over their food.

"Bless this food to our bodies. And help us in our old age, Lord Jesus."

I am touched by the purity of the scene. Their hands clasped together, like country versions of a Precious Moments doll. There is still so much about prayer that triggers me. I've asked God to save my twenty-year-old friend from brain swelling, and God killed him. I've had people pray for me to be healed of my homosexuality my whole life. My mom has said that she prays this every day. I hate that.

But this couple, in a posture of gratitude and reverence, sits here and asks God to help them in their old age. They believe that God, the maker of the universe, is looking out for them. And if they ask Him, if they submit to Him, maybe He'll bless them with a little extra favor. The understanding that this couple isn't in control of everything, and they are taking a moment in a busy restaurant to embrace that truth . . . all of this moves me. And perhaps that's the real meaning of prayer. Not the prayer of asking-for, but the prayer of surrendering-to. Of speaking your wants and needs to the universe, just to know them clearer yourself.

It reminds me of an article I read about "deaths of despair" in the United States in the nineties. The paper tracked the rise in suicides, overdoses, liver disease from alcohol abuse, and the like in white middle-class Americans. They found the rise directly correlated to a decline in religious participation. Without a God to lean on, without your confusing days being written in the stars with purpose and direction, without God having a plan for you and your measly life, many people fall into hopelessness. Human beings need to believe that their strange lives have cosmic meaning.

We order some greasy fajitas. I'm not supposed to eat grease, so I just nibble on the veggies and chicken as best I can. My pain is pretty low today, as if the doctor's words of assurance untied the knot in my abs.

We get back in the car and drive west.

The road stretches far and straight ahead. The forests have been cleared for fields and the hills are not large enough to turn the road off course. It plows forward like an arrow onto the horizon. I cannot imagine the summer heat my mother would've walked through. The misery of it all. Not only the sweating, which I hate, but the heavy backpack. The back sweat under the pack. The newlywed glow and the horrible realization that your fast-wedded husband can be an asshole.

"How did you know how far to go every day?" I ask.

"We would go anywhere from ten to twenty-five miles, depending on the weather and how strong we felt. You think that seeing the road on the horizon means it'll take forever to walk there, but there's so much nature in every step, the sights and sounds, I was never bored. The birds and flowers. It comes so fast."

I look on to the horizon and smile. My mom can still surprise me with her brightness.

We wind through the confusing sprawl of Dallas and enter the wide, big-sky country of the Texas panhandle. A flatness that is rare in the world. A silent ocean made of land.

As we're driving we see what looks like a dead cow on the side of the road. No, it's a pig. It has little high-heel hooves. But it isn't pink. It's brown. A boar. And it's big as a heifer. Bloated with gas, looking ready to pop. Legs pointed out like a porcelain salt shaker. Oh my gosh, this is one of those feral hogs!

I perk up, realizing that I've heard of this phenomenon. An invasion. A menace to this part of the country. I learned about it from a viral tweet in 2019. The nation was debating gun control after mass shootings in El Paso and Dayton, and a guy named Willie McNabb tweeted, "Legit question for rural Americans— How do I kill the 30–50 feral hogs that run into my yard within 3–5 mins while my small kids play?" It became the meme of the week, with tens of thousands of comments and replies and jokes. I remember listening to the *Reply All* podcast episode about it. They explained that while the tweet was funny and easy to mock, it was a sincere question and a real problem. It really did happen to the guy who wrote the tweet.

"Mom, this is one of those hogs that are taking over the country!"

"The what??"

"Feral wild pigs! It's an epidemic. I have a podcast about it."

"Oh yes, let's listen."

I put on the podcast. Mom cocks her head to the side in animated listening.

Pigs are not native to North America. Apparently they were first brought to the continental United States in 1539, when Spanish explorer Hernando de Soto landed on the Florida coast. These domesticated pigs were often brought by explorers and colonists as a low-maintenance and hardy source of food. As Europeans spread around the continent, they left pigs behind or allowed them to escape. These domesticated pigs adapted quickly to the wild, living in swamps and forests and eating anything they could find. Roots. Leaves. Worms. Fawns. Pretty much anything. Then, in the early 1900s, Eurasian wild boar were introduced to North America as an exotic game species for hunting. These ravenous beasts, even tougher than their domesticated cousins, spread in the wild faster than they could be hunted and began breeding with the feral pigs.

Pigs have the highest reproductive rate of any ungulate on earth. Males can reproduce by twelve months old. Females can reproduce at six months old. And with the right diet, they can have two litters a year, with six pigs in each litter.

"Well good Lord," Mom says to the window.

From 1982 to 2016, the feral pig population ballooned from an estimated 2.4 million to 6.9 million, with 2.6 million living just in Texas. Current trends show them at an annual population increase of 18 to 21 percent.

And so, McNabb's tweet went viral because city people don't know anything about this. Twitter seemed to pause that day, so that everyone could make a joke.

"You still wake up sometimes, don't you Clarice? You wake up in the dark and hear the screaming of the thirty to fifty feral hogs.—@notabigjerk"

"The only way to stop a feral hog is with a good guy with a hog. —@arieldumas"

"Take me down to the paradise city where the hogs are feral and there's 30–50. — @nomiddlesliders."

But "rural Americans," especially in Louisiana and Texas, knew.

"That's how it always is," Mom says, shaking her head. "First they make fun, and then they find out we were right."

We see another hog up ahead. Just off the road in the grass. We start counting. Two. Three. Four. We count six hogs. They haven't exploded from hitting a car. They aren't shredded by a Mack Truck. They just lie dead by the side of the road.

As we drive into Seymour, Texas, there are more hogs displayed on either side of the welcome sign. Their placement looks intentional, like a warning. The town is small; we drive through it in a few short minutes. On the other side of town, two more hogs.

We keep counting. Eleven. Fifteen.

The tweet was vindicated. The man was right.

In the distance are windmills, lined up on the horizon like alien sentinels. Tall as skyscrapers, sweeping their blades through the air in the slow motion of giant things. Mom scoffs.

"I don't like these windmills. They ruin the sky," she says.

"Really? I think they're beautiful. They're sleek. They say something about humans trying to do better, make cleaner energy. They're cool."

"I liked the oil pumps," she says.

"The oil pumps??"

"Yes. They remind me of when the west was wild. Hardworkin' people."

She misses the oil pumps? I was raised to see them as bastions of natural destruction. And windmills as harbingers of hope. Maybe she sees windmills as change and the loss of a way of life. They stand in stark contrast to this landscape and what remains. Clean, white, futuristic, looming over rusted trucks and crumbling barns. *The future is coming and it doesn't care about your western stories.*

We are hunting for Gilliland, Texas, a dot on the map where my mom and dad stayed for a week with a couple named Homer and Ruby. Our route is Highway 6, a two-lane paved road running from Abilene into Oklahoma. The turnoffs are equal parts dirt and paved, and we pick one of the paved ones, following a narrow road toward what the map says is Gilliland. The fierce winds of this flat world have blown dust over the road in many places, and there are no tire tracks. The Google Maps entry shows that Gilliland does indeed exist, but there are no photos of it, no gas station, nothing but a dot placed randomly along a country road.

The windmills watch us as we approach from the distance.

"This is wild, like Mars," I say.

"This is real country. Makes you tough. Where real people live, scraping by."

"I don't think real or fake or any people live here."

As we near Gilliland, I see one of the windmills is no longer on the horizon, but here. It grows so high in our view that I have to lean forward into the windshield to see it.

"I've never been right up on one, let's drive up to it," I say. There is no need to look at the map. I see a dirt road up ahead that runs straight to its big white base. I turn right and the dirt is printed with the deep grooves of a bulldozer. Recent. As we approach, the area around the windmill is completely groomed down, a dirt patch the size of a football field, dug up and tilled. It seems to be the diameter of the spinning blades.

The turned-over soil is fresh enough that not one plant or weed has grown. This newness looks out of place. This one area has been cared for, while everything around it is forgotten. As we drive around the stalk of the beast, I see one imperfection in the soil. Something crumpled on the ground. I see feathers. It is gold and brown and white with spots of black. I pull up to it and it is a barn owl. It must've collided at night with the silent killer of a windmill blade, a hundred feet of metal cutting through the dark air with no sound but the woosh of wind. This beautiful technology, saving us from cooking our planet. This dead bird, trying to fly through the air in which its family has lived for a million years.

"Oh I hate that," Mom says. "That beautiful bird. You know I have an owl that lives at our house. I see 'im a lot. He sits and hoots at me. I was awakened by 'im the other night."

"Hooting outside your window?"

"No, he came to the front door. My phone went off, tellin' me my Ring camera detected somebody. It was one in the morning. That scared me, bein' in that house all by myself. Then I looked at my phone and he had landed on my front porch right in front of the camera. He was lookin' right into the camera. Sayin' hi to me. I think he protects me.

"I love owls so much. I bet he is. Watching over the neighborhood."

We drive away and Mom is leaning forward into the windshield, remembering where to go. The few buildings around are dilapidated. Trees are growing through collapsed roofs. The wood siding has turned gray, cracked and flaking. The driveways are covered in grass and weeds. The entire town consists of about ten structures.

"OK, so your father and I were walking through Crowell, Texas, in furnacelike heat when a '76 Dodge pickup pulled up and a cowboy stepped out. A tall man in his sixties said, 'We figured y'all might like a cold drink.' Everybody in a hundred-mile radius knew who Peter and I were because we'd been featured on the front page of local newspapers and every rancher kept an eye out for us. Lots of people set out to find us, driving up and down the highway. Back then there wasn't much excitement in small towns. Anyway, that was Homer, and he let us sit in the cab of his truck in the AC and we were so grateful. Before long he invited us to come stay with him and his wife, Ruby, back at their ranch here in Gilliland . . . which even then was hardly more than a pothole in the road."

We turn off the pavement onto a dirt road that runs south, passing a couple of abandoned homes. Well, I think they're abandoned. A few are deceptively in-between. One shows signs that someone may still own it. But the yard is unkempt, and a car is buried in weeds. A little farther and we pass a stone building, regal with tall windows and castle-like arches. "Whoa, what is this building?" I ask.

"That was a school. Built with FDR money in the thirties," she says, still looking for our turn. "Right here, turn here," Mom says. She hasn't been here or seen the house in over forty years.

We pass an old store with an awning that looks like it might have had a gas pump a thousand years ago. "Wait wait wait, stop," she says and she flips through the *National Geographic* issue. She shows a picture of a smiling old man in a cowboy hat and his gray-haired wife, both holding glass-bottle Coca-Colas in the doorway of a building. "Oh here it is. This is Homer and Ruby, and it's in front of that old gas station right there."

"Wow." I recognize the photo she's showing me. I've seen it hundreds of times before in that *National Geographic*. I look up from the magazine and at the exact door, porch, and white cracked siding. There it is, snapped into the context of the world.

"OK now, turn left here," she says. We pass a few houses, all empty. Mom has her hand to her mouth, squinting at each home. "No, it wasn't this close to the road." We drive slowly by a house standing alone in an overgrown field. The windmills watch us in the distance. The house is abandoned but it's made of brick and looks sturdy. Nothing caving in. Just weeds and young trees hugging its edges.

We park and Mom opens the door, possessed. We have to step high over the tall grass and gnarled weeds. The front door is sealed with a padlock. The windows boarded up. Mom stands in the yard and puts her hands on her hips. "This is the house, I believe. I'm just pretty sure that is it."

"It's abandoned now," I say.

"Oh yeah, well they died years ago. And they built that house. This was their ranch—320 acres of wheat and cotton. They were what's called dry ranchers, because they had no creek or river for a water source. Just rain. They grew cotton, and it came up all the way to this porch. You couldn't have a grass yard on a dry ranch. But Homer and Ruby were in their midsixties when they met us. Never had any children. And they scraped by a hard life out here on the edge of the West. Toughest, best people you could ever find. And they treated Peter and me like we were their family."

On the front porch is a loose brick that has the word *Texas* pressed into it. "I'm taking this as a souvenir," I say. I feel like I need to take something from this moment. My mom is wrapped in a blanket of rushing memories. "I think this is it. It looks different. It's been forty years. No one's been here in a long time." Her tone is reaching for the feeling, but the coldness of this forgotten house, a temple to entropy, quiets her. She squints, as if to say it doesn't look exactly as it should. Or does it? She battles the cruel truth that what we remember does not stay as it was, and maybe never was what you remember at all. Fact overlapping with feeling, exaggeration, and gaps filled with imagination.

I put the brick in the trunk, and we drive away toward Amarillo. Mom's hands are folded in her lap.

It's getting later in the day and we need to find a spot to eat. We enter a town called Childress and there is a Subway, what seems to be a diner, and a Chinese place. We are far from anything, and there is still a Chinese restaurant here. Who must run it? Who do they hang out with? We choose the diner because we always choose a diner. Inside, it is half diner, half bar. The bar is full of camouflage-wearing men with baseball hats, the uniform I've grown accustomed to seeing. Fluorescent lights hang from above and the place is entirely too bright. The office lighting is casting black shadows over faces from hat brims. They all seem to be looking at the TV. A football game. The restaurant side, which we pick, is less crowded and less interesting. Simple booths. A fish tank with pink plastic seaweed. We each order a burger and I look at the map. "I think we can make it to Amarillo tonight, which will put us in a good position to make it into Colorado tomorrow."

"Sorry to interrupt," comes a voice from behind me. A lady with deep wrinkles splaying out from her eyes and the corners of her mouth, lines on lines, stands up from the booth next to ours. Her gray hair is pulled into a tight ponytail. She looks almost stylish. Not from the country. Her face says farmer, but her clothes and demeanor say city. "But Amarillo is 120 miles away. I'd just stay at the hotel right here, connected to this restaurant. I'm staying here."

"Oh, 120 miles is pretty far. Thank you for the tip," my mom says warmly.

The lady shifts to turn her body to us, unleashed by my mom's tone. "I'm driving across the country, from South Carolina to Vegas and back, alone," she says. "I wanted to see Vegas and no-body can stop me. I'm seventy years old and I just got in the car and hit the road."

"Wow," my mom says. "We're driving from Nashville to New Orleans to Oregon then back to Nashville. My son is driving me on the path I took when I walked across America in the 1970s."

"Oh my goodness," she says, frowning and nodding her head, weighing her adventure against ours. "What a special time with your son. I don't think my daughter would do something like that with me," she laughs intensely. "OK I'm going to have a smoke, I'm sorry I bothered you."

I notice that her plate is still piled with food. She's stepping out for a cig midmeal. Addiction is a powerful thing. When the woman has gone outside, Mom leans over the table.

"Do I look like I'm in my seventies?"

"No, Mom. You don't look a day over fifty-five."

"I don't think I look as old as that woman."

"Don't worry Mom, you don't." I hadn't even thought to compare her to my mother. I don't compare my mom to anyone. To me, she is not an ordinary woman who had a child and went on measuring herself against other people, like all of us do. She is my mother. My first god, and therefore the god by which all others are judged. The water invisible to the fish.

Mom finishes her food, stuck in a loop of reassuring herself. "I think I look pretty good for seventy-four years old," she says to herself.

"I think we should make it to Amarillo. I'm happy to drive in the dark for a bit. A bigger town will have hotel options," I say.

"Fine by me, I'm not tired," she says.

WE DRIVE IN THE DARK. I put on '70s classic songs. Mom fiddles with her phone, working on an Instagram caption for the day. The road stretches straight and hypnotic. My mom's face is lit by the glow of her slow typing. We make it to Amarillo by 11 P.M. and check in to a Holiday Inn.

"How is your stomach, honey?" she asks.

"It's actually feeling much better today. I felt so good that I forgot about it."

"See," she says, smiling and raising her eyebrows. "Anointing oil and prayer works."

Another leg of the trip done. We're a few days in, and I take a moment to inventory. I'm enjoying this. My mom is a good travel partner. She doesn't complain. She's full of stories and documents. Her journal is thorough. The route is clear. This is what I hoped it would be.

But I am nagged by the one thing. I want to go deeper than learning about her past. I want to talk about me. I want to know if she's reached a new place in accepting who I am. And I'm too scared to ask directly. And I'm annoyed that I'm scared.

I lie in bed thinking about the cliché of gay men and their mothers. Why is it a cliché? Why are we so often wrecked by, or best friends with, or some blend of the two with, the women who raised us? Why do we obsess over upper-middle-aged actresses and the Real Housewives? Is it because those women are mother-aged, and we have been trained to fixate on the subtle emotions of such women?

When I was younger I obsessed over the genetic reasons for being gay. My youth pastors, my church friends, my mother all believed that it was a "choice" and a "lifestyle," disapproved of by God. I wanted to prove to myself and my church and my mother that loving who I wanted was natural, and therefore God given. Or at least God's fault. I'd say, "I know I didn't choose this. Why would I choose persecution?" They would pivot their argument. "We all have desires that we can't help, and God asks us choose Him over our desires. Death to self. It's not the desire that's a sin. It's acting on it."

My mind wanders in bed. My mother is breathing slowly and evenly now, asleep. She seems so innocent, lying on her side, her knees tucked up, hugging a pillow.

Why am I obsessed with her? And not obsessed with my father?

She looks so harmless next to me, across the nightstand. Why does she have so much power? Why do I care if she comes to my wedding?

There it is. The thought wiggles its way to the top. My wedding. The wedding that may never come. But, what if it does? This is the layered goddam thing, the loop in my mind. I was taught to "die to self," to give up my desires to God and let go. To be celibate. And then I finally shed that story, and allowed myself to want what I want, and love what I love. I can't settle for duty. I want passion. I want libido. I want to be married. I want a husband. But I still beat myself over letting myself want something. And I've been wired to hold my wants with an open hand. Rebrand "God's will" as "the universe" or plain old fortune. It's the same shit. The belief in a plan. I still have that belief. And I fear asking for what I really want. This is my tug against the past and now and the future. Ropes wrapped around each limb, pulling.

Maybe tomorrow I'll ask her. *Would you come to my wedding if I married a man? Would you want to? Mom, what would happen if, or when, I got married? Would you support me?* I practice how the conversation might go, what she'll say. *"Absolutely not." "You know, Jed, I've been thinking, and yes I would." "It's against my beliefs." "I still have to think about it."*

How am I going to bring it up? It will start with acknowledging "THE email" from 2018. The most intense conversation we've ever had, and it was typed, because face-to-face would have been too much for me. Too scary. Too awkward. It started with an email from her.

Well, it started with a podcast interview I did. My first book was coming out, and my friends Ruthie and Miles had me on their podcast. I thought they were going to interview me about my book, which they did, but they really wanted to talk about my relationship with my mother. Much of the conversation centered on "how brave I am" to have the relationship I do with her. How strong I must be to survive her beliefs. The interview was loving, and I thought the questions and conversation were really good. We lavished my mother with praise. But we didn't mince words that her beliefs hurt me. Both Miles and Ruthie know her, though Ruthie knows her better, and they really like her. There was no venom.

What I didn't appropriately consider was that talking about my mother in a public way can be hurtful—for her. And couching our conflicts in "I love her so much, but . . ." doesn't remove the sting. It's condescending. I am talking to thousands of people on a platform that I control. And I'm using her as my foil. It isn't kind to her. It isn't protecting her. She listened to the interview and then wrote me the strongest-worded email I've ever received. She was offended. Hurt that I would make her my talking point and punching bag. Hurt that I talk about her and not my dad, my dad whose sin exploded our family. His sexual sin might be a cause of my sexual demons, she wrote. He should be the villain in this story, not her, the one who sacrificed everything as a single mom for her three kids.

She mentioned an incident that happened with Ruthie just a week before the interview. We were at my mom's lake condo, and a bunch of my friends were there. Mom was serving good food and hosting, as she does. And Ruthie, in front of everyone, asked her, "So, when did you first know Jed was gay? What was his coming out like?" Ruthie assumed it was a sweet story my mom might tell. But it is not, not for my mom. She froze. I wasn't in the room, so I don't know what she said. But my mom dodged the question. And she wrote in this email that Ruthie had embarrassed her. She was angry with Ruthie for so callously bringing that up. She wrote:

> *Every interesting novel, movie, or story has a protagonist and antagonist. Obviously, I'm the antagonist in your "awakening." While readers, friends, followers, and Californians endorse homosexuality, the gay lifestyle, and gay marriage, I cannot massage Scripture to approve of it.*

The quotes around *awakening* turned my face hot with anger. The forensic way of speaking—"endorse homosexuality"—felt so impersonal. So parroted from a pastor. Where was my mother in all that gibberish? Where was the person in there? She continued:

> *That's nothing new, but it hurts deeply that you use your mother as the antagonist to your choices. I understand the ten-*

sion between mother and son make good drama, but you've painted me as a religious caricature. I'm your mother and I have feelings. I don't want to be a focal point of podcasts and interviews.

This embarrassed me. She was right. I didn't mean to caricature her, and maybe I didn't, but she felt that way and I hadn't loved her well.

I'm growing old, and nobody's fool. My heart has been broken and humbled most of my adult life, and at 71, I accept reality and have lived long enough to know I can't change or control anyone. But I have learned that God hears and answers fervent prayer. That we reap what we sow. God is not mocked. I have learned the hard way that there are wages to sin . . .

I've seen her do this before. In Instagram captions and other emails. She starts writing in biblical speak, like a chant. Phrases spill out. It's no longer her words or her voice. It's as if she's reciting a spell.

Jedidiah, the darling of The Lord, I will always love you, adore you, pray for you, and want the best for you.

I Love you with every breath.
Momma

Reading that email sent me into a spiral. I was ashamed that I hurt her and didn't consider her feelings. But I was pissed, too. I was tired of her praying against my sexuality. I was tired of her being devastated that I was "afflicted" with this "curse." And the moment I read that email, I sat down and started typing.

Momma,

I love you so much and thank you for your kindness with me through this. I am sorry for talking so openly about you on the podcast, and for not having the emotional intelligence to understand that it would be hurtful. I am a total open book and an extroverted processor and the division between private and public is naturally confusing for me.

I told her I loved her unconditionally. I told her that Ruthie and Miles didn't mean to set her up as villain. The words were just flying from my fingers.

It's clear to me now that it doesn't feel good to be talked about, especially when it's about someone's hurt and pain, with no ability to speak for yourself. Even though you're lavished in compliments, it's clear that Ruthie, Miles and I are in ideological agreement in opposition to you, and that feels like a gang up, and I'm sorry. I didn't know the conversation would include you and I really am sorry.

As I typed, I realized that I had thought about saying all these things for years. They'd built up like gunpowder.

I don't talk publicly about Dad's sins because they are sad and obviously private and wounding. They tore apart our family. I talk openly about your faith because it's something

you openly espouse. Something you're proud of. It isn't a pri-
vate matter. That is a very different thing.

Also, I have never "felt" hurt by Dad's sins. He hurt our
family. And he betrayed you. And for that, I'll always be
angry with him. I am aware of the destruction he brought to
our family, but I don't feel it, because I was too young. I know
it is better to have married parents than divorced parents. But
apart from that, I had a wonderful childhood and two
Christmases and never felt any of that. I felt love from you.
And love from him. And I was off playing in the creek by the
time I have any memories. On the contrary, the Evangelical
Church hurt me. (I won't say Christianity hurt me because I
don't believe that God or Christ did.) The church traumatized
me. Stigmatized me. Caused me to fear myself. Caused me to
feel rejected and alone and helpless. Caused me to believe
something about myself that I now believe to be a lie.

The keyboard was smoking.

Their interpretation of the Bible, one that selectively
changes Biblical laws with the evolution of culture (like
1 Corinthians 14: 33–35 clearly forbidding women from
speaking in church) and upholds others, e.g., homosexuality.
To me this is worshipping the Bible, denying that it's being
selectively interpreted, and not worshipping the living God.
I talk about that openly because I can honestly trace my pain
to that.

But, put simply, we believe different things about the
Bible. I believe it is a rough road map to God, inspired by
God, full of myths and history, and given to us purposefully

imperfect, so that we would not worship it. We would be forced to seek God through it. This is what CS Lewis believed, who is my favorite as you know. You believe, if I understand correctly, that it is the infallible word of God, full of history and instruction. You believe it must be interpreted and contextualized, but certain things are so clear on their face, that modern contextualization falsifies God's intention. And to approve of what is clearly forbidden is to choose man's wants over God's commands. I don't see it that way. Therefore, we're going to approach it differently and come to certain impasses.

Also, I don't believe Dad's sexual sin made me gay. And I don't search for some dark force in my childhood that turned me this way. I don't feel bad about being gay. I don't believe it's a sin. Indeed, I believe God wants me to be just the way I am. And so, when you say Dad "cursed me" and "what kind of man would say that," I am deeply deeply hurt by those words. You imply your disgust with what I believe to be a fundamental part of who I am: who I love. Not a choice. Not a lifestyle. A primary piece of being.

I tried to believe what you believe. Trust me. I dove headfirst into church. Leading youth groups at USC. Bible studies. I tried dating girls. I sent one of them to therapy because she felt I had "experimented on her pretending to be someone I'm not." I studied gay conversion. I went to an Exodus International meeting. I read every theology book and practiced celibacy for 30 years. I had my first kiss at 28 years old. And I found that commitment to be life-destroying. Soul-sucking. Full of darkness. I asked God for "life and life abundant" and saw none. Only strong signs to the contrary. I have never met one "gay-convert" that radiates light and truth. And I've met quite a few.

Suicide among gay teens is one of the highest suicide rates of any group. People don't commit suicide for other "sins." No one kills themselves so they can continue getting baseless divorces, or to gossip or steal. People commit suicide when a fundamental part of who they are is being destroyed, and it is better to not be alive than to be a hollow shell.

And when I speak about this stuff, I don't mean to imply that you hurt me. It's the church and the beliefs that hurt me. You have raised me, protected me, built me, encouraged me, fought for me. You are my champion.

But I can remove myself from those churches and those specific beliefs. But I can't remove myself from you. Or my history wrestling with this. Or my childhood story. It is all intertwined. And I have to talk about it and write about it and process it.

I love you more than any other person in the world. And it is a deepest wound to me that I can't share such an important part of me with you. I wish I could share my life with you. I've had two boyfriends. I've been in love. I've had my heart broken. And I've never been able to celebrate or process any of that with you. I hope to find love again. I want to get married. To a man. The "best" day of my life. And you probably won't be at the wedding. I'm sure you wouldn't want to go. I want to start a family. And when that happens, I won't feel comfortable around you with him and our children. And therefore, to honor my new family, coming home for holidays will end. Of course I'll still see you and visit, but alone and at

different times, and a huge part of my life will be quaran-
tined. We'll talk about other things and I'm sure get along as
we always do. And if that's all I get, and all you get, we'll
make the most of it. But I am not going to change. I am not
just gay. I am proud of being gay and believe it is part of my
God-written story. My calling. I feel affirmed about it from
God daily. From every direction. The only place in my life that
is not affirming is you.

I had not realized this until I wrote it. She is the last place in
my life that matters to me that doesn't accept me as I am.

If Dad had said the things you've said to me about my
sexuality, I would not have a relationship with him. I would
have cut him off years ago, hurt and broken. But he hasn't.
Neither has Rebekah (we talk openly about my relationships
often), or Luke. Or anyone. But you raised me. You made me.
    I am still in a relationship with you because in spite of the
pain those beliefs have caused me, it is worth it. I'll never
wall myself off from you. No matter the cost to my heart.
    I don't want to wreck your faith or your view of the Bible.
It's six verses. But I believe they are written by man, not God,
or perhaps by God, instructing a way of life two thousand
years ago that has changed. God spoke through Paul and the
prophets to instruct specific churches in a specific time. MANY
of the lessons are timeless. Many are time specific (in my opin-
ion). There are many denominations of Christian churches that
now affirm gay marriage. Their deacons and elders studied the
scriptures and came to the deep belief that God affirms these

unions in the modern context. The Presbyterian church. The Episcopal church. The United Methodist church. The Evangelical Anglican church. The Evangelical Lutheran church. The Alliance of Baptists church. Those are a few of many.

I've certainly entertained the belief that I could be wrong. I was completely motivated by that belief from 13–30. And then I couldn't do it anymore. I wonder if you could do the same.

To believe that maybe the church got this one wrong, or that God will understand if we all got it wrong, as I'm sure there are things that we've all got wrong in history. What if God really intended for women to be silent in church. And as most aren't, is God weeping, or patient with us and understanding. Do those above denominations have it wrong, and therefore is their faith counterfeit and insufficient? I don't know.

If your conviction is unmovable, and these verses are the hill that are worth dying on, then I must say they are where I will die too. I am completely convinced in the rightness of my path, and so, when I am married and happy, that will be a major part of my life separated from our relationship. That is sad, but I understand if that is where you must draw the line.

I will never stop laughing and loving life with you. I will never stop celebrating you. I will never stop spending time with you unless you ask me to. I am your adoring son. Your biggest fan.

I feel convicted to talk about my journey with faith and sexuality to the public. But I will seek to protect you, and minimize when I speak of you specifically, and when necessary speak only praise of you, and not hurt you or make you feel caricatured. I am sorry for when I have failed at this in the past.

> *Forever yours,*
> *Jed.*

I hit Send and waited. I had never spoken so directly about these things. Some reflex came over me. I couldn't tiptoe anymore. I was willing to blow it all up for my truth. The three hours I waited for a reply were weeks of time.

Then she responded.

> *Jed,*
>
> *There's so much here to digest that I'll have to let this settle awhile, and read and re-read several times. This is such a bittersweet letter. Thank you for responding and hearing my point of view about the podcasts and interviews, and sharing yours.*
>
> *Love you always and with every breath,*
> *Mom*

She said, "read and re-read." Wow. It feels good to be heard. To pour your heart out and get thoughtful consideration.

But there was one more conversation I needed to have. And it was going to be on this trip. *You're almost forty years old. Get a grip and be a man.*

I am looking at her asleep in the bed, her eyes closed and body quiet. Such a small thing, breathing in, breathing out. She hugs her pillow like a little girl.

4

· · · ·

We wake up just before dawn, the sky slashed with yellows and pinks. It is 20 degrees outside. I didn't know Texas would be cold like this. We pack up, and as I go out to the car to get it warmed up, I see the large diesel truck next to us is running. Fumes creeping from the tail pipe in thick, milky poofs. Inside the truck is a young boy, in his early teens. He is sitting alone and the music is blasting. I recognize it immediately. The soundtrack to *The Shawshank Redemption*. The Thomas Newman score, with its heavy swelling strings. This thirteen-year-old boy, exactly the age I was when I was obsessed with film scores, is sitting in a truck at 6:30 A.M., feeling his feelings to the finale of *Shawshank*.

Something feels very warm in me, seeing that. An intense sense of affection, of belonging in the world. As if our personalities are melodies in the universe, transposable into different keys. I am being made everywhere. Or, I am an element, not an individual.

The car heats up, Mom loads in, and we back out of the hotel parking lot. It is Friday, which means I'm excited because it's New Music Friday on Spotify. A little weekly treat, a playlist of brand-new stuff that I can sift through and see if I discover any gems. I notice a new Charli XCX song. "Ooh I wanna hear this new song," I say to Mom. "I'm gonna play it, OK?"

"OK honey, whatever you want to listen to," she says.

I start playing it. It's hyper and gay and fun.

"Your dad and I walked into New Mexico in late summer and it was so hot I thought I would die, and your dad was always ..." She's talking and talking and I'm trying to listen to the song. I pause it, thinking she'll notice that I'm pausing because I want to hear it and don't want to simultaneously listen to a story. She doesn't notice.

No New Music Friday for me. She's now reading me an excerpt from *The Walk West*.

As we drive through the last of Texas, we pass a billboard that says "Serve the Poor." It does not advertise anything. There is no church name at the bottom, no follow-up billboard with a number to call. Someone has paid for it to say "Serve the Poor" and nothing else. In Tennessee, I've seen billboards with Bible verses and commands to follow Jesus. Warnings of hell. In Los Angeles, I've seen billboards that say "Black Trans Lives Matter." But here on the plains of Texas, the message isn't condemnation or fire or justice, but service.

"I like that billboard," Mom says. "What do you think the difference between 'help the poor' and 'serve the poor' is?"

"Hmm . . . I don't know. Help seems like giving them something once? Where serve is more of a lifestyle?"

"To me, it's about posture. Help puts you above the poor. Serve puts you below. It's better to lift up the poor and treat them as Christ in disguise. So you put yourself below them and serve them."

"I really like that."

The flatness of Texas gives way to the dribbling spillover of the Rocky Mountains in northwest New Mexico. The land begins to roll, barely rising, and then seemingly out of nowhere, Mom sits up. "It was around here we first saw the Rockies," she explains. "And I was so overcome. It felt like a real achievement." In every direction you could see the soft flow of grassy fields. "I remember walking with your dad and coming around this exact bend, the first time we saw the Rockies, and it was the most incredible feeling. I was so desperate to be out of this hot, flat country. And the mountains were like a gift from God. Of course, when we saw them, we were still days away from reaching them. I remember right about here antelope came right up to us. It was surreal. Let me find a passage," she opens her books and hunts.

"Here we go . . ." She begins reading my dad's part. "Almost a blur of yellow tan and white, they stopped and looked at BJ in the eye, they were no more than 30 feet from her. The three of them played for about half an hour and then it began getting hot. The antelope followed another mile or so, stopped, turned toward Apache canyon, and ran full speed. Maybe the prairie had given us a gift for giving it a chance. Maybe the antelope were young and foolish. Maybe we'll never live long enough to forget what happened."

Right then we see a herd of antelope in the distance, standing in golden grass. "Look right there," she says, proud of having manifested them.

And like magic, we crest an upward slope that's so gradual I don't even notice it, and then we see them: a white-capped wall on the western horizon. Mountains. Far away. Maybe thirty miles or more, but very much there, and very much a surprise. I didn't realize how much the Rockies extended into the northeastern corner of this state.

The mountains get closer and we can feel a shift. Texas is gone. This is something new. A different "West." The topography is reaching up in drama. The road follows a river into the crook of two mountains and now we are beneath them. "We can stop in Red River for food. I remember Red River," Mom says.

The town sits on the river and is built for tourists, with ski rental places and winter gear shops. Hotels and gift stores. We find a big brewery for lunch. It has shiny tin walls and giant fans, fourteen feet wide, hanging from the industrial ceiling. TVs are on every wall. There seem to be thirty beers on tap. The waitress comes and I order a Caesar salad with chicken. My mom orders a salad too. Mom explains, "We're ordering salads because my son has a stomach issue, a food allergy or something gastric, and I'm ordering a salad because I'm fat."

She needs to apologize for not ordering burgers and bread.

We eat our fill and get back on the road, headed north through ski towns I didn't know existed. We wind through pine trees and shaded pockets of snow, climbing higher and higher. Mom has a swelling excitement about her. She is happy to be in the mountains. "I just, OK, when we see Colorado, the sign, we've gotta get a selfie of us going into Colorado where I was attacked by out-laws," she says.

I laugh. "OK, OK."

But we soon forget our mission and the Colorado sign sur-prises us around a bend and whizzes by.

"Oh dang it!" she exclaims.

"We'll have other opportunities," I tell her, which doesn't make sense, but I don't want to turn around. The land opens up to wide flatness, an ocean of sagebrush with jagged mountains far north in the haze of distance.

"It was right about here that I got chased by the outlaws. Just over the border into Colorado."

"OK, what happened again?"

"We were on this lonely road going to San Luis, the wildest part of Colorado, and this is the road where we were attacked by a carload of renegade outlaws who tried to run us off the road. We had to jump out into the sagebrush and lay low all night long while they went up and down this road searchin' for us."

"What were they saying?"

"They said, 'Señorita we're going to kill you!'"

"They said they would kill you!?"

"Yes, more than once. And the sheriff, we went into town the next day and told the sheriff and he said he knew exactly who they were. They were a band of outlaws, and he had shot and killed their leader just a week before."

"Good Lord, Mom."

"They tried to run over us several times. We had to hightail it off the road and we went out in the sagebrush and they came out in their car screaming they were gonna kill us. We ended up sleeping out in the sage. We hunkered down in a low place and slept without putting our tent up.

"One of the life lessons I learned was that when you are faced with an attack, that kind of danger—I mean, wildlife teaches us that you get away from it, and you hide and be very still till the danger passes. So we hunkered down and slept on the ground that night under the stars while these outlaws went up and down the road looking for us."

She leans back in her chair, letting her lesson resonate in the car.

"Wow Mom, did Dad try to protect you?"

"Not really, we just hid. There were more of them than us, and they were big and clearly drunk. I don't think he could've protected me if he'd wanted to."

"Hmm," I said, picturing them holding each other on the ground, afraid to fall asleep. Adrenaline subsiding into exhaustion, and then fear springing their eyes open at the smallest crunch of a twig. I've heard her tell this story before. But it feels more real, seeing the place now. The scariest thing that has ever happened to her, maybe, being hunted by drunk rapists, has become a favorite story she likes to tell.

We drive north through the plateau of southern Colorado, empty and wide enough to fit Los Angeles in it, and then turn west toward the San Juan Mountains. These are the sharpest mountains in Colorado. The most rugged and steep. Right in the center of the San Juans is the town of Lake City, where my mom and dad spent the winter of 1977–78. They couldn't walk through the Rockies during winter, and a man in Texas had told them of a rancher who would give them a place to stay and wait out the coldest months. As we wind up over Slumgullion Pass, Mom looks out the window at every vista, searching for something specific.

"This is the exact stretch of road where the photographer from *National Geographic* came with us to take photos for the magazine. It was fall colors, September I think. We had to reach Lake City before the first snowfall, so it would've been September, October. And the photographer got a wonderful photo of us right around here somewhere."

We wind from switchback to switchback, climbing the San Juans. "Here! Here, pull off here!"

I veer onto a dirt pull-off. A grass meadow slopes down to a wall of pines and aspens. But there is an opening, like the parted sea, with a long valley between tall mountains, perfectly framed. And in the valley, a winding river shimmering in the afternoon sun. "This is it!" she says. We hop out of the car. She is looking at it through her iPhone, stomping through the grass. I walk to the tree line and pee. "This is exactly it," she says, disembodied and reflecting. She snaps a few dozen versions of the exact same photo.

Back in the car, she reaches into the back and grabs the blue binder. In the pocket is the *National Geographic* she was talking about. She flips through and finds the shot. I see it now. There they are, my mom thirty years old, my dad twenty-six. Their backs are to the camera and they are small in the frame, dwarfed by the bigness of the river valley. They are wearing long, cream-colored pants and everything else is obscured by the size of their packs. They stand confidently, each with one leg cocked, as if claiming the land. The grass is gold then as it is today. They are young and married and in love and midway through their great walk across America. A photographer is following them around. They are on the upswing and they can feel it. She runs her fingers over the photo in the magazine.

We crest the top of the mountain and begin our long descent into the valley of Lake City. As we reach the bottom of the switchbacks to the valley floor, Mom is looking for a sign. "There was a monument to a famous cannibal around here. He was a con artist. It was right by this bridge." There is no sign. I drive slow and she is craning to see. "They must've taken it down. It was an unbelievable story."

"Oh I love a cannibal. What did he do?"

"Lemme look up the Wikipedia." She puts on her glasses and googles. "Let's see, Lake City, cannibal . . . yep, there he is. 'Alferd Griner'—Greener, I don't know how to pronounce that middle name—'Packer, January 21, 1842–April 23, 1907, also known as 'The Colorado Cannibal,' was an American prospector and self-proclaimed professional wilderness guide who confessed to cannibalism during the winter of 1874.' See, yes, he got stuck in the snow and ate the other guys!" She keeps reading, "'He and five other men had attempted to travel through the San Juan Mountains of Colorado, during the peak of a harsh winter. When only Packer reached civilization, he said that he had been abandoned by his party, but eventually confessed that the party had resorted to forced cannibalism of dead members to stay alive when they became lost.' Oh, I just love these old mountain stories."

"Mom, I love how morbid you can be," I say.

"It's just such good stories. People were tough back then in the real Wild West."

We drive along the Gunnison River and before we reach town, Mom is looking closely out the window again, trying to find the cabin she and Dad lived in. The rancher they stayed with was a man she calls Vickers. He owned hundreds of acres around Lake City and ran cattle on the hills. Now we drive by a place called Vickers Ranch that seems to be a collection of rentable cabins. "Right there, here, pull off here!" We turn onto a little street named Hummingbird, and across the narrow river valley, just on the other side of the flowing water, is a small log cabin. "That's where we lived. That's where we wrote *A Walk Across America*. Your dad wrote and I rewrote and edited."

"Did the Vickerses own it?"

"Yes. And right there, we lived in that cabin with my little red Volkswagen bug."

"How'd you have a car if you were walking across America?"

"We'd stored my bug with friends in Dallas. So Peter flew down and drove it up so we'd have a car for the winter. It had been mine in Louisiana. I loved that car. One time I drove it off a bridge."

"You did what?!"

"I wasn't drunk or anything. I fell asleep. I had my friends in the car, too. It wasn't a high bridge. But I drove right off. Whoops."

Just beyond the cabin is a ridge, a wheat-colored cliff looming above the river. "Right there is the land your dad and I bought. Four acres. They split it down the middle when we divorced. I wonder if your dad still has his."

"He does," I say. I've asked him about it before. Now that I'm here, feeling the history and the holiness of the place, I want to put a cabin on that land.

"Let's drive up to it," she says. I back the car up and head toward the ridge.

All throughout my childhood, Lake City had been her dream in the distance. If a road trip took us through mountains, or any topography that rose above flatness, she would mention Lake City. "One day I'll build a cabin on that land." As if to reclaim the dream of the mountains that the divorce had tainted. To bring her children here to play in the golden fields, in the snow, in the aspens. She held on to that parcel while she clipped coupons to save thirty cents on breakfast cereal. While she learned to connect our pop-up camper to the sewer at the campground, so that we could go on vacations as a family.

And then it happened. Mom ran out of money. I was in law school at the time, and I remember realizing that I would need to make a lot of money because someday I'd have to take care of her. I would be her retirement plan. She was planning to sell the farmhouse, the one I was brought home to from the hospital, the one my parents bought and renovated together. After the divorce, my mom moved us up to Nashville, thirty miles north, and rented the house to a series of families. I was a kid, so a lot of these details are blurry, but I know the renters were often a headache. She rented to friends of friends, and her desire to be a kind Christian woman got her in trouble. There were months of unpaid rent. Fights and lawsuits over money owed. Then countersuits. This rent was my mother's livelihood, and it was always a mess.

The farmhouse sits at the corner of a freeway off-ramp and a highway that runs into the town of Spring Hill. It is a highly trafficked and therefore valuable spot. After a long run of failed renters, an investor came along wanting to turn it into a commercial development, with the farmhouse at the center of a planned shopping center. She refinanced the mortgage again and again, pulling out cash to pay for plans and designs and architects. And then that deal fell apart. She was out of money. Out of refinancing options. No renters.

It was either sell the farm or let go of Lake City. Burn one dream to save another. Mom had planted a garden of hopes in the '80s. A beautiful farm in Tennessee and riverfront property in Colorado. Now the garden was fallow. What "could be" withered. The decision impossible—which dream to kill.

Then, unsolicited and right on time, some doctor offered to buy the Lake City land. Out of nowhere. My mother, running on fumes and coupon codes, took it as a sign. The real estate agent who contacted her gave my mom some convincing advice. "This land might have been your dream. But you have adult children, and they're going to have children. And this isn't their dream. Getting the whole family to this remote place even once a year will be a chore." This logic made a lot of sense to my mother. It was her dream, not her children's. She accepted the offer and sold her dream away.

I don't know what it meant for her to sell. I don't know what it means to loosen the grip on a dream after it's already in your hands. I suppose it depends on what hope the dream held within it. A chance to reclaim what was lost? To know that the life you had wasn't totally destroyed?

We wind up the hill and I pull the car onto a dirt driveway that leads to the two properties. "Hasn't been touched since we bought them," Mom says. "Looks exactly the same as the day we got them."

"Should we get out and walk around?" I ask.

"No, that's OK," she says.

She purses her lips in thought.

Throughout all her money problems, my mom talked to God. In times of poverty, she'd speak of having patience with God. About God's timing. How His ways are beyond understanding.

She watched my dad make gobs of money in real estate while she clipped coupons. She quoted Job: "Why do the wicked prosper, growing old and powerful? Do they ever have trouble? Does God distribute sorrows to them in anger?"

I think letting go of Colorado loosened her grip on the farm, too. Before long, she decided it was time to sell—if not the farmhouse itself, then the land around it. She knew the farm next door had sold to a hospital. Maybe she could get them to buy her land, too.

Instead of putting it on the market, she contacted the hospital directly. I don't know how one does that, but she did. My mother has always been good at tracking down a phone number. They said, "You're not going to sell to Maury Regional, are you?" This was their direct competitor. My sweet mom said, "I don't know what I'm going to do. But I'd love to keep this from becoming a bidding war and adding more stress to my life. So if you make me an offer, we'll see if we can get this settled."

They offered seven figures.

She took it. She got to keep the farmhouse she'd raised us in. And she sold the thirty acres around it. It left her with enough money to have a good retirement. To pay off her mortgages. To be debt free. To afford a plane ticket and a restaurant meal every now and then. She even bought a little diesel RV, to drive the Blue Ridge Parkway. To visit Colorado with her friends.

She could probably afford to buy back the Lake City lot now. But that doesn't seem to be of interest to her.

Why am I telling you this? My mom's business? Because it's the world I grew up in. I was raised knowing that empires fall. That my parents published very successful books, and then the publishers stopped calling. That they were rich when I was a baby, but not when I was a teenager. That credit cards get declined. That we shop at Burlington Coat Factory and TJ Maxx because the mall costs too much. That we only buy used cars because new cars lose $10,000 in value the moment you drive them off the lot. That our dog Coco is old and the vet is expensive, so Mom drove him over to Papa's house and he shot him in the head and buried him in the woods.

I learned that your dreams for your life might change and die. That your agent can dump you. That the farmhouse you bought to live out your fantasy might become a place of great pain, a grave-yard. And then, a saving grace—the pain of losing the thing you love can be the very thing that saves you. All that prayer, all those promises from God, finally answered.

We drive away from the ridge and back onto Highway 149 toward the main street of Lake City. Crossing the river, I see the beautiful cliff of the lost land on the other side. It has no idea what it meant to my mom. And now to me.

More houses and a few lodges come into view. Lake City has no ski resort, so it's missing the fat injection of wealth that you sense when you visit Telluride or Aspen. It has a few attractive Victorian homes, a lot of simple farmhouses and cottages, a couple motels. There is a park in the center of town. A few restaurants. One art gallery. "OK go slow go slow, turn left here," she says, directing me through the tiny grid of the town. Perhaps five streets by five streets. There is a pale yellow church and a rectory house beside it. "This is the church we went to."

The town is riddled with UTVs and dirt bikes, their combustion engines echoing through the canyon. Twenty of them parked outside of the breakfast café. It's evident that without a ski resort, the tourism industry here has adapted to motor sports and off-roading. To gas-guzzling Mars Rovers ripping around the mountain passes.

My parents' time in Lake City ended when enough snow melted for them to hike over Engineer Pass to the town of Ouray. A helicopter could get there in ten minutes, but the wall of mountains is formidable. Driving the twenty miles by car takes more than an hour, and that's if the road isn't muddy.

Back in August, when I came to Colorado with Mom and Glenda, we drove over the pass. We rented a jeep and went backwards, from Ouray to Lake City, the opposite direction of Mom and Dad's walk. The road starts as carved rock on the edge of a cliff. Immediately you're driving along a deadly drop with a creek flowing below. After several intense rocky navigations, where Mom and Glenda got out of the car in case I flipped it (which I almost did), the road crested to a high plateau of ponds and pines and aspens and mud holes. Then more boulders in the road. It's so high up that no trees grow. Even in August, snow hangs out in every shadowed place. I couldn't believe they walked across this. It was on top of these mountains, during that walk, that my mom lost her footing and slid a hundred yards down a glacier. As she was about to fly off the edge into an ice ravine, her backpack snagged on protruding ice and she was saved.

That drive, more than anything else, was what ignited my desire to take this trip with my mom. As she held on to the "oh shit" bar in the Jeep and we crawled over the most treacherous road I've ever driven, my seventy-four-year-old mother was ecstatic. Fearless. Telling me to hit the gas. Thanking God for the scenery. Upon seeing a horse on the side of the mountain, she rolled down the window, her iPhone capturing everything, "Oh praise God for the beauty of this world, and the eyes to see it, and the body parts work!"

It's November now, so we can't drive Engineer Pass again. We'll go north to Gunnison, sleep there, and continue to Salt Lake City. Gunnison, while not strictly on the path of their walk, was a big part of their winter in Lake City. They made weekly trips there to stock up on groceries, eat at restaurants, and pick up friends from the little airport.

We leave Lake City, following the Gunnison River up the long valley.

"Right here is where a man drove off the road and died," she says. "It's been so many years, but I can still see him in my mind. I believe his last name was Hall. He and his wife ran The Sportsman. Fell down into the canyon." The road traces the edge of a rocky cliff with short blips of railing but mostly nothing to stop a car from launching down the hundred-foot cliff. It seems that they added ten feet of railing right where Mr. Hall flew off. The rest is still wide open.

Mom points out to a meadow. "Your dad and I went on a date night out there, where some locals told us about petroglyphs in the rocks. We went out and found them. Incredible."

It's strange to picture my parents, ten years younger than I am right now, on a date night. Kissing and laughing. I've never known them in love. But a whole world existed between them before I did.

Winding from river valley to valley, my mom points down into a steep canyon. "That is Black Canyon Road. It makes Engineer Pass look like a ten-lane highway. Dangling right off the cliff. We did that years ago. Terrifying. You and your friends should do it next time you're here."

I'm looking down in there and the road is thin as a pencil. I cannot imagine driving on it. I don't think I could. And my mom did it and loved it.

Why would she tell me to do that, but tremble every time I travel to Mexico or some big city? Maybe there's a chasm between the fearlessness of her childless youth, her memories from then, and the fearfulness of a protective mother.

We enter Gunnison at twilight, and Mom says she's craving a "nice" burger. As we wind into the town, the whole place looks new and clean. Buildings of glass and steel. Freshly bulldozed lots ready for expansion. It appears to be one of the pandemic boom-towns. Colorado has a lot of these. Places where city people moved when the world migrated to phones and Zoom. They wanted out-door space, natural beauty. They wanted Colorado. And they had big-city money. So these little mountain towns experienced a gold rush of gobbled-up housing. This in turn created a housing crisis for the ski bums and local twentysomethings who no longer could afford rent. Which led to restaurants closing and limiting their hours, because no one could wait tables and still live in the town where the restaurant served all these rich people.

We drive past a restaurant with big garage-door windows and newly framed walls. It is packed with people. "People means it's good," Mom says. I pull into the gravel parking lot, tires crunching on the gravel.

Inside, the people all look the same. White. In their twenties and thirties. Flannel shirts and baseball hats for women and men alike. Wind-chapped faces, pink and cracked. The men have well-kept beards. The women wear no makeup. They signal to each other that they love the outdoors. They hate big corporations. They hate gentrification. They hate Trump. They love a big mutt rescue. There are several shaggy dogs lying on the concrete floor. Before Instagram became a way to publicly signal, these are the people who loved bumper stickers.

I like these people, despite their conformity. They seem happy. Laughing together and pleased to see each other and drinking flights of beer.

I'm ready for a crowded place after being alone with Mom all day. I assume there will be a long wait because the place is swarming, but I spot one empty table in the corner. A waitress sees me eyeing it and points with her head, mouthing over the noise of the room, "Take it." We sit and scan a QR code for the menu. I want something healthy, so I order a beet-and-kale quinoa bowl. Mom orders some other bowl. I am still not drinking alcohol, but I want a beer so bad. Beer feels obvious in this place. But I don't get one. A small victory of willpower. Mom orders a "Coca-Cola please." The bowls come quickly and they taste good.

Mom is on her phone, scrolling through her photos and videos of Lake City. She watches videos she took out the window, the wind screeching through the phone's speaker. Normally that would make me die, but this restaurant is so loud with people, it's fine. Ish.

"I wish I'd got a beignet in New Orleans," Mom says. "I've been thinking about it ever since."

"I bet we can find one. Maybe in Salt Lake. I should've just done a U-ey."

"I do want something sweet. Eating this healthy quinoa"— she pronounces it *kwu-no-ah*—"I'm still hungry."

The young waitress circles by to check on us. "What sweets do you have?" Mom asks.

"Our special dessert today is a beignet."

My eyes widen in shock. Mom is delighted. "Oh perfect, I would love one! Jed, you want one too?"

I cannot speak. What the hell. Mom seems hardly surprised.

"Uhm, no, I'll have a bite of yours," I say.

"It's really delicious, it's really authentic," the girl says.

"Oh yay!" Mom clasps her hands in joy. The waitress shuffles away and I slap the table. "Mom! You manifested that!"

"It's meant to be," she says calmly. "God gives us a little wink sometimes."

I know it's only a pastry, but my healed stomach pain, her anointing oils, and now this damn beignet. Whenever God answers one of her prayers, it feels like a little defeat. Like "there she goes again." God is on her side. She is giving God the credit for everything good and for being her teacher through every obstacle and blaming the Devil for every deceit. She sees the divine drama playing out everywhere because she's looking for it, and what a salve, to believe everything in the world happens with intention.

But, pragmatically, it works.

Ugh, it works.

The beignet arrives and it is beautiful. The powdered sugar gets all over us. We relish it.

We've been on this road trip for four days now. Seeing only each other. Talking only to each other. Normally, spending too much unbroken time with my mother activates my flight response. But now we're ending day four, and I'm . . . enjoying myself. I like talking to her. I like hearing her stories. Even when she reads to me from her book or her notes, I gobble it up. Maybe it's because I know I'm going to write about it. The curiosity of the journalist diffuses the nature of the son.

Mom is looking for our hotel reservation in her emails. It's not coming up. I glance over to her phone. The font is huge, thanks to her aging eyes. And I see her inbox. I just see the subject line. "China Invasion Imminent, how to prepare!" "Voter Fraud Proven!" "Real Republican Daily" and "Daily Prayer For Patriots."

My mom is a conservative, but also an individual. If the government says something, she wants to believe something else. If a pastor says something she doesn't like, she'll read the Bible herself and articulate her challenge. She is the queen of "doing her own research." This usually comes in the forms of health remedies. Colloidal silver. Chemicals in our foods. Diatomaceous earth. 5G radiation.

She seems like she would be a prime candidate for QAnon, but I've made fishing statements around her and she has scoffed at the absurdity of it. Thank God. What is the tipping point, where a conservative becomes alt-right? Why does someone listen to Rush Limbaugh and Sean Hannity, but not InfoWars?

And what could be said of me? Why do I love Michael Barbaro but don't watch Rachel Maddow?

Well, I can tell you. I appreciate at least the veneer of good faith, an acknowledgment that the other side isn't peopled with cartoonish devils. I don't really see that in right-wing media.

I do have an interest in dissidents. My mother believes 5G may harm us, and I think she's silly. But what of the nonconformist who warned back in 1940 that cigarettes kill? What of the contrarian who said the CIA was spying on Martin Luther King, Jr.?

I mean, I've seen no evidence that 5G or the Covid vaccines are harmful. But have I done that research myself? No. I just trust the media would tell me if they were. My media. Whatever media my mom is consuming, they're quoting "research, studies." They're slinging medical articles and YouTube videos of doctors saying that mRNA vaccines kill. A month before our road trip, she sent me one of these videos. It's a clip of a longer talk, but even the clip is twelve minutes long. "Something to consider," she wrote in the subject line. "Doctor calls out deadly vaccine!" Twelve minutes is annoyingly long for something I instinctively discredit, but short enough to give it a go. So I do.

It's a doctor on a stage with a PowerPoint. He has studies and graphs and lists of ingredients in tiny fonts and words like "embryonic stem cells." I write my mom a long response.

"OK I'm six minutes in and here are my thoughts: he's using a lot of technical science speak that is above my pay grade. And so, what I'm doing is I'm trusting the lingo of an expert. That's what I have to do in a world that requires a minimum eight years of school. When experts disagree, my only recourse is to trust more experts than less. When 98% of experts agree about something, and 2% have something else to say, who knows . . . history may pan out and those 2% are right, but in the face of the current evidence, and the current expertise, I'll choose to go with the preponderance of evidence. Covid hospitalizations and deaths have completely plummeted in states with high vaccination rates. So, I get it, if there's something in you that absolutely doesn't want to take the vaccine, don't take it. But I totally understand why the United States government, the entire Trump administration, the vast majority of health professionals, and the vast majority of scientists support the vaccine and from what I read every day, the evidence is clear that the vaccine saves lives. All I can do is trust the consensus. If there is a secret truth that comes to be that the vaccine causes mass deaths, then that's how it is. But I just don't see the world in a conspiratorial way."

I try to articulate it all in a way that engages her. I don't care about winning the argument. I want her to get vaccinated and be safe.

She responds, "Just wanted to share another scientific side. Time will tell, as Papa used to say."

This enrages me.

I mean, what if it turns out my mom is right? What if they discover some unforeseen side effect that doesn't show up for ten years? That everyone who got a vaccine dies, and only those who stood firm survive? Evolution will select for their stubbornness. Right?

But the way I'm wired is that I trust scientists and experts. I don't believe that everyone is lying, or that power corrupts all minds beyond reliability. It all makes me dizzy. How can I debate someone who starts with the belief that they're being lied to, or that God's plan will save us from ourselves? What is the point of argument?

And yet we argue. Because even with different footings, one must still know what to do next. Should we cross the river or not? Should we eat the strange berries because we're starving, or could they be poison and it's too risky?

My analogies are rudimentary. The modern world is not. We are debating things that require expertise. If I argue with my mom, and she tells me that a forty-page study says vaccines kill and then another study says lockdowns hurt children, am I supposed to go read those studies top to bottom before I respond? Let's say I lob a point-by-point rebuttal, with other studies that I've subsequently read. How do I establish that my study is from a credible source while hers is not? I'm sure this is possible. Debate doesn't seem to work. What does work? I don't know.

"Oh here is the reservation!" she says. "It went to my spam!"

We pull up to the big Comfort Inn and head inside. The man behind the counter has a dense, black mustache, a crisp white shirt, and a golden name tag. He greets us with a heavy Indian accent. "Gudevening," with a showman's grin. I go to the bathroom while

Mom checks in. I return to find her showing him her Instagram. "He has a brother that lives in Columbia!" she says to me. She shows him photos of the small town where I was born in middle Tennessee, of the farmhouse where I grew up.

"It's become a beautiful restaurant. The post-and-beam ceiling is gorgeous, a huge stained-glass wall that I had commissioned is in the big dining room that was the kitchen. Getchur phone out and I'll put it in, you have Instagram?" she says.

"Yes ma'am, I do," he says.

She takes his phone, slides her reading glasses onto her nose, holds the phone at just that mom distance, and begins typing with one finger. "Here it is," she says, handing it back.

"Oh, it looks beaudiful."

"Yes, have your brother go there. The food is delicious, they have a world-class chef. Reba McEntire eats there."

He is smiling. Is he enjoying this rapport or waiting for it to be over? I can't tell. He hands us the keys to our room. "I put you in our biggest room," he says.

We go up the elevators and the room is gigantic. Not in a luxurious way. In a converted conference room way. The beds are a mile apart. The TV is two miles across the room. The first half of the floor is tile; the second, carpet. "What kind of room is this!" Mom shrieks.

The bathroom door doesn't exactly close because it is a barn door on tracks that just slides over the doorway.

"He gave us the biggest room. It isn't exactly fancy, but I'm grateful. This is nice," she says, unpacking her toiletries and nightgown.

"Mind if I take up the bathroom for a minute?" she asks.

"Not at all," I say, and she shuffles in there with her bag of things. The sliding barn door doesn't close properly, and leaves a couple inches visible. I watch her fight the door. I can feel the strangeness. I should not even have a millimeter of visibility into the bathroom. What if she wants to use the toilet? I turn the TV loud so she can assume I'm distracted. I choose to be distracted.

There is weirdness in the air.

I never hear the toilet flush. She slides the barn door open and her face is glistening with oil.

She sits in bed, kicks her feet up, puts on her reading glasses and takes her phone into both hands.

"Shew, my feet stink," she says. "They don't tell you that when you get old, your feet stink."

5
. . .

We wake up in Gunnison to a neon-pink sunrise. The high-altitude clouds like Bob Ross brushstrokes. It is 19 degrees. I go start the car and let it run for a while to warm up. Today we're aiming for Salt Lake City or even Twin Falls, Idaho.

We drive down from Gunnison into a huge valley just north of Montrose. As we exit the San Juan Mountains, the aspen trees and lush green grass end abruptly and the land becomes dry, a mix of white and pale pink. Then the pink fades to gray, leaving only rocks and shrubs. By the time we've passed Grand Junction, heading west to Utah, it is almost hard to see. The rock and sand reflect sunlight through every window. The buildings sitting out in the vastness are cracked and often abandoned.

"This was one of the hardest stretches of the entire walk," Mom says.

"Why?"

"Well at some point, and I mean this is not very pretty, but at some point I was close to heatstroke, it was 108 degrees, and we found a drainage ditch and I drank out of it. Within fifteen minutes, I was sick as a horse. And it so happened a highway patrolman drove by and saw we were in trouble and stopped to help us. He took us five miles up the road to a motel and dropped us off and I threw up all night long."

"What do you think was in the ditch?"

"Oh, well, cattle urine, bacteria, and just parasites and who knows. I got so sick I couldn't walk."

"Wild, Mom. I can't believe you drank out of a farm drainage ditch. That's so intense."

I am again amazed at all my mom and dad survived. She holds up a photo of them lying under their umbrellas on the side of a sandy, rocky hill, the exact spot we're driving through now. The land hasn't changed at all in forty years.

"Once we get to Green River, I think your dad and I turned north from there up Highway 191 to go to Salt Lake that way. Yeah, see here it is on the map." She holds it up to my face.

"Mom, I'm driving," I say, annoyed. "I'll stop in Green River and then I'll look and we'll find it."

"What should we listen to today?" she says, bubbly and moving past my scolding.

"You know what I know nothing about? Butch Cassidy and the Sundance Kid. I've never even seen the movie."

"One second," she says with the tone of a detective, typing Butch Cassidy into her podcast app. "Let me seeeee." She theatrically scrolls down the list of options. "Here we go. Found one. It's just one episode, but it's an hour long."

"Perfect, lets listen."

Butch Cassidy was born Robert LeRoy Parker in 1866, right after the Civil War. His story is the story of the end of the Wild West. As the nineteenth century came to a close, the profession of the cowboy was ending, but the lore was alive and well. And Butch Cassidy became a living legend, a folk hero, against that backdrop.

Getting the true history of Butch Cassidy isn't easy, because the newspapers exaggerated everything. Butch was reported dead more than fifty times over his career, and none of those reports were true. One writer said that there were five Butch Cassidy clones roaming the west. The legend became bigger than the man.

What we do know is that he was born in southern Utah. He told people he was from New York City, but that is one of his many flavorful lies. Mormon missionaries recruited his parents to move from England to Utah, uprooting their family to cross an ocean and live as subsistence farmers in a land with little rain and few people. There would be no crops left over for sale. What they grew, they ate. Their ambition in life was to settle Utah, be Mormon, and survive.

As Butch grew up, he wanted more. In the 1900s there was a popular saying: "Go see the elephant." A reference to the itch some people felt to get out and see the Wild West, to go to the frontier, or even just the big, wide world. Cassidy wanted more than the simple life of a Mormon farmer.

He had the American compulsion to get out and break away and see.

"That's how I felt in Poplar Bluff," Mom says. "I got that itch, I knew I couldn't stay there."

"*Go see the elephant*," I say. "That's cool." I make a mental note to google that later.

He first broke the law when he was thirteen years old. He rode into town to buy overalls and the general store was closed, so he broke in, took the overalls he wanted, and left a note. "IOU I took the overalls and I'll come back. —Robert Parker." The owner didn't like that, even if the kid had left a friendly note. He called the sheriff, and the sheriff went to their little farm and told his father to watch his boy. Butch was mad. He had been kind, wrote a letter, and said he would come back with the money. And he still got in trouble. From then on, Butch had a disdain for rules.

He started stealing cattle and horses. Which got him arrested and sent to jail. But he was so charming, so well liked, that one of the men whose horse he stole wrote a letter asking for leniency. The judge liked him too and let him out after six months.

"That would happen to you," Mom says, smiling at me.

"I'm scared of getting in trouble, I could never be a criminal," I say.

"You'd be a good one."

Butch was free and went back to thieving. Soon he'd gathered a crew of clever criminals and they called themselves "the Wild Bunch." There was a clear self-aggrandizing element to their intentional branding, but it must be said: in the world of criminal arts, Butch was brilliant. He perfected the idea of a "relay" team. Every robbery ended in a chase. To beat the lawmen's horses, he would put sprinter horses at the front and stage slower, long-distance horses a few miles away. He and his men would sprint the first leg of the chase, throw their loot onto the new horses, and ride off as the sheriff's posse lost steam.

They robbed with an unwritten moral code. Butch's rule: Don't hurt anyone and don't rob from the little man. Rob only from the banks. When they would hijack a train, passengers would take off their watches and offer them out of reflex, to which Butch would say, "We don't want your money, we want what's in the American Express safe." To go along with that Robin Hood ethos, Butch was famously charming. Women loved him. You can't learn to be charismatic or even teach yourself. You either are or you're not.

"I agree with that," Mom says. "Your dad was very charming like that."

In 1899, he became a superstar after his robbery of the Overland Flyer train in Wilcox, Wyoming. The Wild Bunch blocked the tracks, escorted everyone off the carriages, and filled the car with dynamite. They used too much and blew up not only the safe but an adjoining train car full of raspberries. This burnt a lot of the money and also dyed much of it red with raspberry juice. In spite of the excessive explosion, they made off with gobs of cash.

A few years earlier, news of this robbery would only have spread on horseback, town to town. But something new had entered the West: the telegraph. The morning of the robbery, the telegraph alerted newspapers and sheriffs all across the West. It was the beginning of the end for the western robber. Information now moved faster than a horse. It was harder to escape and disappear into the forgetfulness of the plains. The Wild West was being tamed.

"That's almost sad," Mom says.
"They were criminals, Mom."
"It's the loss of a way of life."

By the turn of the century, Butch had grown too famous. In 1901, he and his partner—Harry Longabaugh, the Sundance Kid—headed to the new wild west: the wild south. First Bolivia, then Argentina. They went down there to disappear and try something new: to be honest ranchers. But going straight wasn't as easy as they hoped. They swung back and forth between law abiding and law breaking. The grass was always greener. When Butch got clean, he got bored. By 1905, they were back to robbing banks.

Was he a ladies' man? Yes, in a way. He certainly charmed them. But there are scholars that make a case for him being gay. The evidence is piecemeal: He was nicknamed "Sally" in the family. He never, in all his life, had a girlfriend. In his letters from South America, he made a big pretense about saying he was a ladies' man. He wrote about all the whorehouses he frequented, writing and speaking in a way that didn't seem like him. As if to combat rumors.

I am looking straight ahead at the road, but my periphery is watching her. I can feel her listening. I am looking for cues of disapproval. Of scoffing. "Why does every historical figure *have* to be gay?" she must be thinking. Or is she? Podcasts were meant to be our safe place, our noncontroversial place. But nothing can be kept out of the room forever.

What did it mean to be homosexual in those days? Men outnumbered women in the west thirty to one. You weren't seen as purely homosexual if you had sexual relations with a man. They called it "mutual solace." It was not talked about much, and it wasn't judged as it would be later and in other places. Most historians believe that Butch and the Sundance Kid died in a shootout in San Vicente, Bolivia, across Argentina's northern border. On November 6, 1908, a police patrol discovered them hiding in a rented hut one night, and a gunfight ensued. In the morning they found both outlaws dead, shot in the head. It is assumed that, rather than allowing himself to be captured, Cassidy shot Sundance and then shot himself. Apart from stories and word of mouth, we have no direct evidence of this event. No one identified them when they were buried, and there are no photographs of the bodies.

One historian claims Cassidy survived the shootout, had plastic surgery in Paris, married, and moved to Spokane in 1910. Well into the 1940s, eyewitnesses claimed to have seen one or both of them. People around the world did not accept their death. They wanted the story to continue. "Butch must've come back and outfoxed everyone," they thought. It wasn't unusual for famous outlaws to have impersonators and imposters going around claiming to be them.

As one newspaper historian put it, "When the legend beats the facts, print the legend."

COLORADO GIVES WAY TO UTAH, and it is true desert. Cottonwood trees line the rivers. Some are hanging on to their yellow leaves from fall. Many have lost their leaves altogether. I cannot imagine walking across this. Almost no shade. No towns for miles and miles. Finally, Green River approaches on the horizon, a town whose name may suggest a pastoral oasis, but it is not. It is named for the color of the river that twists through the cracking desert.

"Finally, civilization," I say as we pull off the exit into town.

"This is where your grandparents on your dad's side—Mary Jenkins and Fred and their youngest girls, Betsy and Abby—came to spend time with us on a family vacation."

"How did they find you?"

"We'd planned to stop here in Green River and spend a week in a motel and rest. The desert heat was too much and it was such a welcomed break. Remember, Peter hadn't seen his parents since our wedding on February 7, 1976, meaning two years. So they drove out from Greenwich, Connecticut, and Mary burst into tears when she saw Peter. He looked like a charred lobster and that was hard for her to see."

"I remember Grandma Jenkins being the sweetest lady," I said. "I'm sad I never got to know her, really."

"She was an angel. The Jenkinses lived in Connecticut, which is green and lush, and Mary had never been west of the Mississippi River. People didn't travel back then like we do now. It was a big deal to drive across the country. The sun-dried settlement was an overwhelming culture shock. It was like seeing a different planet. Mary was in her fifties then with clear blue eyes, translucent skin, blond hair tied back in a bun, and she had the spirit of a dove."

"I think I was fourteen when she died, my memories are blurry around it all. I have fond memories of her but I don't remember her that well. I just remember her smiling and being very loving."

"Oh, her sense of joy and excitement were pure and childlike. I had never met a woman with such a transparent and wonder-loving personality, and I adored her from the first time I met her. There were parts of Peter that were just like her and made me love him even more. She was a radiant flower and a symbol of dew in the desert."

I wish I had known her the way my mom did. How many interesting family members do I have that I know nothing about? Great-grandparents. Great-greats. On my dad's side, I'm sixteenth-generation American, meaning my family came here about as long ago as possible for Europeans. How many of their stories are lost in the recesses of my DNA? I guess many immigrants came over poor and desperate, so losing the past might have been a relief. All these years later, I barely know my family two generations removed.

We find the road that goes up the eastern side of the Wasatch Plateau. Highway 191. The mountains we drive beside are different from the San Juans of Colorado. They are less woodsy. Drier. Balder.

Mom sits in the passenger seat, flipping through her notes from the walk. "Oh, listen to this," she says.

"OK, so we're in Price, Utah. This is from my original notes from August 5, 1978: 'My youth, my sense of pride in my looks. I'm 31 years old this month and I feel 100. Where can I find relief? I'm so deeply unhappy, my skin is rough and already lined with wrinkles.'" She stops and laughs.

"Oh God," I say, laughing too.

"Young people are so stupid," she says.

"We'll be in Salt Lake by lunchtime," I say.

"Salt Lake is where I got hit by the car. I hope we can find the cemetery."

We wind out of the mountains and see the big desert valley that holds the Great Salt Lake and the cities that blur together into the city's metro area. Provo. Ogden. The mountain pass at the top is littered with giant windmills. As we enter the edge of suburbia, Mom sits up. "Right around here is the burger place your dad and I stopped at. It was the first sign of civilization in a long while, I remember it!"

The clarity of the memory is a surprise to her. She didn't know it was there. She didn't plan to look for it. But the sight of those mountains opening up into the giant expanse unlocked that burger joint just below the surface, a few millimeters away, perhaps, in the neurons of her brain. A pathway paved forty years ago that hasn't been pulled to consciousness since I've been alive. But there the memory sat, swirling as electricity in her brain, waiting . . . and then, flash, she knew. "Just around this bend, you'll see it. It has a big red sign, if it still exists. But I think it was old even when we went there, so who kno— THERE IT IS!"

A vintage-looking roadside diner. I turn in to its cracked parking lot. It's bustling with people. "Should we get a burger?" I ask.

"No, I just wanted to see it up close."

Sometimes a look crosses her face that is close to pain, but softened by sweet distance. Her brow slightly crimped. Eyes warm but glazed. A Mona Lisa smile. Looking deep in thought or sadness, but wholly accepted and no longer crippling. Something like, "Oh we were so in love then, weren't we," or, "It could've been so different, but we've come so far." I've seen the look a few times on this trip. I'm seeing it now.

"You sure? We could get a burger, it looks popular."

"No, that's OK, let's keep going."

We drive on toward Salt Lake City. "Wow look at all this growth!" Mom says. "This might even be more than Nashville!" The entire eastern side of this mountain range has grown together into one sprawling metropolis. "When Peter and I were walking, there were big stretches of fields between towns. Now it's one big city," she says with wonder.

Most of the construction looks new. The houses look cute but 3D printed, exactly the same design in rows and rows. Two stories. Pitched roofs. A young tree by the front porch, freshly planted. Every few minutes, at almost every freeway exit, is a cluster of new office buildings. Glass-plated and shining, as if freshly Windexed. I wonder how the growth of the last decade will look with forty years' distance. When I am old, will a "two-thousand-teens" or "twenties" house have such a clear fingerprint that we'll roll our eyes? I actually like much of the home design these days. Not the apartment design, though. So many of the buildings look like a child stacked them together, like alphabet blocks. Red, yellow, blue squares haphazardly stuck onto white rectangles. They look fast and cheap.

It is November. Many trees are bare, though a few hold some yellow leaves near the bottom. The air outside is chilly. Mom is looking at the map. "OK, so with all this growth, it might be hard to find the exact spot where I got hit."

We drive an hour up the sprawl, moving north from the city of Provo. "I know it happened in the town of Sandy, Utah. Do you see that on the map?"

"Yes, it's about halfway up toward Salt Lake."

"It was Highway 71."

I search "mortuary" in Google Maps, and three show up, all along the exact highway she said. We drive to the first one. "No. This isn't it. I remember it was after a big, long uphill. It was mid-day and it was really hot, and Peter always said we had to walk against traffic for safety, so no one would hit us from behind. But I was so hot, and the right side of the road had shade, so I walked on that side, up a really long hill. Peter thought I was dumb for doing that and told me I shouldn't. But I didn't care. So I walked slowly up a long hill, and just over the hill is where a kid hit me going full speed."

"Funny that we can't blame him for texting like we would now."

"Back then, it was blamed on changing the radio."

We pass another mortuary, but it has no hill preceding it. "Nope, not it."

Then we see in the distance a long upward slope. "It was just like this," she says. "Is there another one coming up?"

"Yes, just beyond."

"This must be it. Go slow." She's staring at every building, hoping a hidden piece of memory will jump out and cause her to recognize something. Everything is Starbucks, Subway, CrossFit, and Fantastic Sam's. Nothing is coming up. But the slope of the hill is.

We crest and then there it is, the mortuary. She is disappointed. "It had this grand entrance, a grassy hill, some kind of big building." We're looking at a stone entrance with a wrought-iron arch over it. It looks old, and it is completely surrounded by shiny new apartments. The Victorian house at the entrance has weeds growing in the cracks of its parking pad. The paint is chipped. One window has particle board over it.

We pull in, park, and get out.

This place looks like it was holding on for this moment. Prime real estate, surrounded by growth. But it's more than a mortuary, it is a graveyard. I suppose it can never be built on. I ask Google, "Can graveyards ever be developed into something else?" It turns out that large cemeteries, which this one is, have various ways of staying alive. Some sell a portion of the plot and create an investment fund for perpetual lawn care and maintenance. Others fill up, run out of money, and default to the municipality, whose responsibility it becomes to mow the grass. Small family plots that are over a hundred years old, of which there are many on ranches and farms and in forests, are virtually unregulated.

"This must be it," she says, "but I don't remember the entrance looking like this. Maybe it was right here that Winky and I landed." Winky is the nickname for my dad's little sister, Winifred.

"Aunt Winky got hit too?"

"Oh yes. She was thrown straight up in the air like a volleyball. She shattered the car's windshield and bounced to a landing fifteen feet away. And I flew through the air and landed in a pile on the grass. This must be the grass. It looks different."

"Well, forty years have passed, Mom. Even if they changed it ten years after that happened, it would be thirty years old now. And memory isn't real. You've told this story so many times, it must've warped over the years in your mind."

"You're right."

"So, what happened exactly that you remember? Did you hear tires screech?"

"No, the kid was pretty young, maybe twenty. He hit me at the bottom of my backpack, and thank God the JanSport packs had a steel frame. I flew through the air and landed here, I guess right here, in this grassy part by the entrance. I opened my eyes and saw it was a mortuary. Apparently while I was lying there in the grass, people came to help. A witness told Peter that a pickup truck cut off a kid in a '74 Chevy and the car was forced off the road and ran into us. The backpack saved my life. I was so bruised up that I couldn't walk the next couple days. But other than that, I was totally fine."

We walk around the space. She is looking at the grass, the arch, taking photos, not completely satisfied. Neither option is good: either she is mistaken, or her memory has distorted the place beyond recognition.

"Well, this must've been it," she says. "OK, let's try to find the place where we saw the Jedediah Smith statue!"

"That was in Salt Lake?" I asked.

"Let me check my notes." We get back in the car and she flips through her journal. "Walked 8–10 miles today to Kaysville. Both of us perspiring heavily. Higher humidity than usual, overcast, windy, and stormy. Saw memorial sign for Jedediah Strong Smith, a trapper and pioneer of 1820's, strong Christian (not Mormon) who ministered to the mountain men with a Bible in one hand

and rifle in the other. Want to name our first son Jedediah. Means 'Beloved of the Lord.'"

I marvel at the way she wrote her journal. The language she used is telling. Like a real explorer. The details revealing of what she found important.

I grew up hearing the story of my naming. My parents saw a statue of the first man to cross America on foot. Of course, they must've meant the first white man, but the color wasn't specified. Hearing Mom recite from her journal, it sounds like it was a plaque, not a statue. Funny how it grew over time in the storytelling. Mom swears it was a statue. That's what we're looking for.

Jedediah became Jedidiah because that is how it is spelled in the King James Bible. "Beloved of the Lord." I was named for a western fur trapper who crossed the country on foot, and now I am the first person in my family to move west and settle there. How much prophecy does a name hold?

I hope it is a statue we're looking for. I want to see the thing that spoke to my mother, that said, "Name your son after this man." I want to imagine what stirred her soul when I was nothing but an idea.

We drive north through Salt Lake City proper, toward Willard, a small town north of Ogden. She says the statue was right off the highway, same one as the mortuary, because that is where they would've walked. We drive slowly and find a little town square. The buildings look fresh. Clean. The old ones repainted or updated. The road recently repaved. "It really should be right around here somewhere," she says. "He was holding a gun. Bronze."

She remembers a large statue now.

"Maybe they moved it," I say. "Maybe it's in this little green square." I point to a nearby park on Google Maps. "They could have put it here. Let's look." We drive a few blocks over. No statue.

Mom is really straining in the passenger seat. Twisting to inspect every inch of this park. It isn't here.

The mortuary was a maybe. A probably, even. This is a nothing. I'm disappointed. So is she.

It makes me wonder if returning to history is worth it. If it's better to live in stories, in the memories that feel big and important. Either the statue is gone or she doesn't remember. Both sad options. And in the meantime, this place has moved on. It doesn't know that it shifted her life and named me forever.

We revisit the past because we want to believe that what shaped us lasts forever. It does not. This is helpful for those who have trauma, and tragic for those returning to remembered beauty. I guess you can't have one without the other. Change is either fast or slow, and it is all there is.

WE GIVE UP the search and head north, to Twin Falls, Idaho. The sun is setting over the shallow marshiness of the lake. We've been in endless suburban sprawl, and now the north side of the lake is open fields divided into sparse farms and homesteads. "Is this what most of this area looked like when you walked through?" I ask.

"Yes," she says, dejected. "You can see how much it's changed. It used to look like this. Now it's all parking lots."

We stop at a diner off the highway as the golden hour makes the world beautiful. It is packed with people, evidence that either there aren't many restaurants up at this end of the lake, or this is the best diner for a hundred miles. We take the very last booth. There is a table of men in the middle. They are wearing Carhartt overalls, but not in the way that's become chic now. They are real, the reason Carhartt is Carhartt. They look like they've been out hunting. They all wear bright orange beanies, camouflage jackets or sweatshirts, and khaki-colored overalls. They are perhaps fathers and sons, or some blend of friends and family. The ages range from twenty to sixty. At the end of the table there is a cluster of twentysomethings. The young ones are attractive. The older men are heavyset and regal, leaning back in their chairs to make room for their bellies.

I imagine what it would be like to join them. Would they like me or distrust me? If I said, "I live in Los Angeles," would they wall me off? If I said, "I live in Nashville," maybe they'd be more open. What do I really know of these people? Maybe one of them is closeted or doesn't even know that he likes men. Statistically, one of them does. At least one. I'm feeling their lives. How little they notice me. How much I notice them.

Mom is writing an Instagram caption. I look at her and feel happy. I still do not have the woolly itch to get away.

We finish eating as the last of the daylight dims. The horizon is dull pink, the sky above almost black. We could stay here or drive the two hours to Twin Falls in the dark. "Let's just go!" she says. "If you're up for driving. I'm awake. I'm happy to keep going. Besides, I don't really remember much between here and Twin Falls."

"OK," I say. "Think we can find a podcast about Jedediah Smith? Learn about him as we drive?"

"Yes I do," she says.

Mom doesn't find what we want, so she reads me the Wikipedia page.

"'Jedediah Strong Smith (January 6, 1799–May 27, 1831) was

an American clerk, transcontinental pioneer, frontiersman, hunter, trapper, author, cartographer, and explorer of the Rocky Mountains, the Western United States, and the Southwest during the early 19th century. After 75 years of obscurity following his death, Smith was rediscovered as the American whose explorations led to the use of the 20-mile (32 km)-wide South Pass as the dominant point of crossing the Continental Divide for pioneers on the Oregon Trail.

"'Coming from modest family background,' blah blah blah—" She scrolls down the page, then continues.

"'Smith led the first documented exploration from the Salt Lake frontier to the Colorado River. From there, Smith's party became the first United States citizens to cross the Mojave Desert into what is now the state of California but which at that time was part of Mexico—' Oh wow, this is why you love California. It's in your name. 'On the return journey, Smith and his companions were likewise the first U.S. citizens to explore and cross the Sierra Nevada and the treacherous Great Basin Desert. In the following year, Smith and his companions were the first U.S. explorers to travel north from California overland to the Oregon Country. Surviving three Native American massacres and one bear mauling, Smith's explorations and documented travels were important resources to later American westward expansion.'"

She looks up from her phone, her head nodding in obviousness. "I believe naming you was a prophecy over your life."

"Probably was," I say. I feel both proud of being named after a hypermasculine explorer and gross that my namesake began the great white Manifest Destiny expansion.

"Hmm, OK. 'Smith informed Eaton that he was completing a map of the West derived from his own journeys. In May, Smith and his partners launched a planned paramilitary trading party to Santa Fe. On May 27, while searching for water in present-day southwest Kansas, Smith disappeared. It was learned some weeks later that he had been killed during an encounter with the Comanche—his body was never recovered.' Wow."

"That's crazy," I say.

"What a legacy. Well, who knows where that statue is."

"I bet it's at someone's house." I smile as I picture it. At the home I rent in Los Angeles, there are two handprints smushed into the back patio's cement. Little hands and two names. Jess and Tyler. This house was home for those children, so much so that they pressed their hands in the cement to say *we were here in this moment* forever. And now they are off somewhere, maybe the same age as me, and I know nothing of them. Nothing of their memories. The house is mine for now.

In the same way, the statue or plaque or whatever it is sits somewhere, perhaps in a landfill. And here we are, looking for it to be forever for us.

We reach Twin Falls and sleep in a weirdly gigantic Comfort Inn. Maybe it doubles as a convention center. It has an indoor pool that is swarming with teens and their chaperones at 10 P.M. There must be a sports team staying here. Mom and I move into our room and she turns on *Ghost Hunters*. The hosts of the show have their hands full of gadgets and are looking for the paranormal in old houses. "Do you ever watch these shows?" she asks.

"Absolutely not."

"Ooh, I love them. I don't know if they're real. But I can believe it."

Mom does her nightly ritual, puts on her big glasses, and climbs into bed. She grunts and makes theatrical noises in her movement. I brush my teeth and get into bed. I have no intention of watching the ghost show, I'll just scroll on my phone. By now, my ab pain is basically gone. Only the shadow of a pulled muscle in my stomach. But I find myself wishing Mom would lay her hand on my stomach again and pray. I want to feel that again, the warm hand of the universe uniting with my feelings. My brain knows that I don't believe an anthropomorphic God cares about my ab. But my little boy heart can feel God's power surging through Mom's praying hands.

What if I got what I wanted, and Mom renounced her evangelical interpretation of the Bible? What if she said, "I've been deceived," and woke up into the mystic confusion of a world without God? Would I be happy?

I would be sad. My mother's certainty is her strength. To see her weak and confused would devastate me. There is a reason existential crises tend to fall on the young and middle-aged. They still have time to build another worldview on which to stand.

I watch her watching TV, and I feel the distant affection of a god, watching from a cloud, pleased at all of creation being just as it is. I know I won't feel this way all the time. But I feel it now.

"OK this show is dumb," she says. "I'm gonna watch my baby elephants." She turns off the TV.

Oh yeah, I think. *Go see the elephant.* I remember, and google it.

"The phrase *seeing the elephant* is an Americanism which refers to gaining experience of the world at a significant cost. It was a popular expression of the mid to late 19th century throughout the United States. . . .

"The phrase may have taken on its American form in 1796 with exhibitor Jacob Crowninshield's Asian elephant display in New York City. . . . A young, 8-foot tall animal was shipped from

India to become the first live elephant exhibition in America. It drew visitors from as far as Pennsylvania and Virginia, making 'I saw the elephant' into a famous claim of worldly experience."

Or maybe it arrived in a more general way. Traveling circuses were common, and you could imagine people saying, "Well, did you see the elephant?" As in, did you see what you went to see?

As America pushed westward, the *elephant* saying merged into a symbol of going west and seeing what promise was out there. "All hands early up anxious to see the path that leads to the Elephant," wrote settler John Clark in 1852. Another westbound traveler wrote in early June 1851, "Some of our company did not lay by and have gone on they are anxious to see the elephant I suppose."

As the great journey progressed, the brutality of the wilderness overtook their optimistic dreams. Travelers died of disease. Dead ends and bad maps led to despair. The reality of the elephant was not what they had expected. In 1850, Pioneer George Bonniwell wrote, "This is a trying time to the men and horses. I have just been to get grass, and got up to my 'tother end' in mud. . . . First glimpse of the Elephant."

The elephant became a joke, a kind of scapegoat for their troubles. The wonder that had spurred their excitement was shifting. Lucius Fairchild, a Wisconsinite on his way to California in 1849, wrote: "That desert is truly the great Elephant of the route and God knows I never want to see it again." In just a few months and several hundred miles, the symbol of their wonder transformed into an image of their disenchantment.

Poor elephant. It never promised to be anything other than what it was.

6

· · ·

IN THE MORNING Mom wants to drive just west of Twin Falls and find a house she stayed in for several days. "Jack and Lucy Ramsey." She says her hosts' names with great fondness.

We drive out over a flat expanse carved with giant gashes of river. Huge mountains give bearings in the distance. We find the little town of Filer, Idaho, and start searching its gridded streets. "It was a boulevard, the nicest one in town, with a median, it was a big ol' brick house." The place feels tired, like all the youth have moved away. We find what must be the street Mom's looking for. It does have a median, but the homes are modest. "I guess this is it," she says. We drive down and her arm shoots up to point. "Oh, that's the only brick one. Yes, two stories, hmm, that's it. It seems smaller than I remember." The house is charming, but certainly not large. "Maybe I'm wrong. But that must be it."

We continue west through Boise and into Oregon. Our goal today is Bend. We cross the Oregon border and it isn't the Oregon most people think of. It isn't the verdant chilly rain forest. It's dry golden fields and pine-covered hills and mountains. It's western. The land looks cooked.

If we wanted a straight shot to Bend, we would take Highway 20, but Mom is insistent that she and Dad didn't walk that way. "We have to go through John Day. I remember it was"—she scans her folder with the printed-out maps—"this one, Highway 26, through Unity and John Day. Yes, that was where I was in the white-out snow and I was about to give up, collapse in the snow. Right there I came upon a baby doe and it looked at me, with peace in its eyes, a sign from God, and telepathically told me to hang on, not far to go. Ten minutes later we were picked up by Mary Lou Koto."

"Who was Mary Lou Koto?"

"She had read about us in the papers. All the local papers ran stories when we came through, so, like I said, it was normal for people to just go out driving looking for us. She found me right after seeing that fawn and told us that there was a local church just up the road that was ready to help us. Get us warm and give us shelter. And she asked if we wanted to spend Christmas Day with her family."

"What a woman . . ."

"I never in a million years thought I'd spend Christmas with a Japanese family. Mary Lou's mother washed and massaged my tired feet. They were such good kind humble Christian people."

We turn off Highway 20 and veer north on Highway 26. I can tell by the squiggling road on the map that we are heading for hills and possibly mountains. The next biggest community is Bend, but there are little dots of towns throughout this giant expanse of eastern Oregon. John Day is there, halfway to Bend. Have I been here before? The hills and dry grass ping something. I remember this road. Yes. This was where my dad and I rode motorcycles back in 2005.

When I graduated college, he finagled a couple of giant Yamahas, Harley Davidson–looking beasts, and we went on a big father-son adventure across the West. We planned for me to meet him in Manhattan, Kansas, at the dealership. We'd get the bikes and head west to Florence, Oregon, where he and Mom finished their walk across America. Then we would take the coast down to Los Angeles, and I'd begin law school at Pepperdine. It would be a five-week trip.

I met Dad in Kansas, I forget how. I must've flown into Topeka. We picked up the bikes and rode the three hours west to St. Peter. This would be our only time on the interstate. I was terrified. I had taken a motorcycle license course in Los Angeles. It was fun. But those bikes were small, almost clown size. This was a 750-pound tank. I was terrified, but we drove slow and deliberate.

Dad's best friend, Skip, had lived in the Bay Area for a long time. He co-founded JanSport and had showered our family with free backpacks since before I could remember. But he was from west Kansas, and he grew tired of the city. He moved to a small farming town, St. Peter, that had been shedding inhabitants for decades. Population: 12. A big brick Catholic church and rectory stood well-built and beautiful on the prairie. The church sold it to Skip for pennies. There were no stores, no groceries, nothing but a few houses and barns and a big old church. The world was flat in every direction and the roads were dirt.

We stayed in that "town" for four or five days. I remember

watching from the front room of the rectory as a storm came rolling over the wide fields. A cloud system as big as the apocalypse, with branches of lightning curling around cloud towers. "This should be called Big Sky country," I thought. "The sky is all there is." In St. Peter I practiced riding and shifting gears and maneuvering the heavy monster of a bike.

One day I went out for a solo ride, and about thirty minutes off into nowhere, I crashed while driving through a mud puddle. The top layer looked dry, but the entire middle of the road was a murky swamp, and I went into a skid. The bike fell on top of me, pinning me to the ground. The mud was slippery enough that I eventually wiggled out, but I could not lift the bike. I wasn't strong enough and there was no traction. I saw the church in the distance and started walking. But this was west Kansas, and it turned out that I was twenty miles away. After an hour of walking, the church didn't seem to grow larger. Finally a man and his wife drove by on a massive tractor and saw this mud-covered zombie walking down the road. Not one car had passed. Not one sign of life until now. I told them I was in St. Peter and they nodded, grunted, waved me into the tractor, and drove me back. They didn't say much to me. They didn't seem used to talking. The man said, "You're not from around here, are you?" which was almost too cliché to believe, but I swear he said it.

They brought me back just as my dad was suiting up to come look for his lost son. The story got a good laugh.

Anyway, we left St. Peter and headed west to the ocean. Our rule: no freeways. Only two-lane highways and small towns and diners and shitty motels. It was a perfect road trip. We went through the sand hills of Nebraska, through Yellowstone, Jackson Hole, southern Idaho, and into Oregon.

And we took our motorcycles on the road I'm on now with my mother. I remember my dad mentioning they had walked that route, but back then, my parents' marriage and past was a foreign language to me, a far-off myth.

At one point, we stopped in one of these cute little towns on Highway 26. Dad and I were walking down the sidewalk to a diner or café for lunch. I was wearing tight jeans, as was the style in 2005.

An entire baseball team was walking toward me on the sidewalk. Even at twenty-three, a bunch of fifteen-year-old boys terrified me. Moving down the sidewalk like a pack of coyotes, laughing at anything weaker than their jokes. My dad must've been somewhere else, using the bathroom or something, because my memory of what happened next is very alone. The front boys pointed at my jeans and started cackling. "Are you a girl? Are those girl jeans?" Someone else said "Faggot" under his breath but loud enough to be heard, which got a hearty and chaotic laugh from the other boys. I didn't say anything. They swarmed past me like bees and kept laughing and were gone.

I don't remember feeling sad. I remember protecting myself with superiority. I classified them as redneck zit-skinned illiterate trash, incapable of surviving in a real city, a real place, incapable of contributing to the world in any meaningful way. I pitied their small-town life. Their townie futures.

But here I am, sixteen years later, remembering it. Crystal clear. As if it just happened. As I drive with my mom down this same stretch of road, I dread seeing that sidewalk again.

The road is two lanes, mostly empty, and we approach large mountains accented with snow in the northern shadows. Up ahead is a giant endless field of sagebrush. A few cows. A couple farmhouses separated by endless nothingness. I am once again reminded how big the United States is, how empty so much of it is. Not empty like the Tennessee countryside, which is sparsely populated but parceled into human-altered tracts of farmland, barn, fence, field. The West is empty and raw in a different way. Of course, every square mile of desert is teeming with its own life and history. But nothing like the East.

Mom holds her phone out the window, filming the approaching mountains. I imagine the poor microphone hissing from the roar of the wind. Tonight she will play it back at dinner, watching the video full volume with pride, ignoring the screeching of the audio. She doesn't care. She is thrilled. "This is the kind of experience that makes me feel alive. I think when I get to heaven I'm gonna have an entire mountain range."

I pull over and ask Mom to get out of the car. I want to take a photo. I have her walk out into the middle of the road, a long straightaway that cuts through the expanse toward the tall mountains. I film her walking away. I say turn around. Snap snap snap. The land is massive, swallowing her up in cinematic bigness. She takes little cute steps in my direction. Her small white shoes. She is fixing her hair, smiling. "Now this is prosperity, to have a life full of adventure and family and nature!" she says, raising her hands in praise.

We get back in the car and Mom asks to see the pictures. She zooms in on her face. Seeing if any of them are OK. "I like this one," she says, showing it to me, happy with her smile and the angle. "You can post that."

We reach the mountains and begin passing through little towns. I, per usual, am immediately enamored by this relatively undiscovered place. Already excited to get on Zillow and imagine my life moving here.

The town of John Day is a blip, one little street. It has a tiny main street with only a few businesses, but our attention perks up when we pass a thrift store with antiques and knickknacks cluttering the window. It says "Paul Knightly Winery," and another sign advertises "wine tasting," even though this is clearly an antiques store. The facade is all windows and I can see a wonderland inside: deer antlers and paintings and lamps and quartz and walls of books. "Ooh, look at that," Mom says. "Wine tasting. I want to go in there!" I flip a U-turn, which is easy because there are no cars anywhere. We pull up, and the closer we get to this store, the more excited I am. It is overflowing with old things.

We open the door to the jingle of a bell. There are fossils and crystals sitting on tables and in display cases. Every inch of the room is occupied except for the narrow paths winding through it all. There are towers of old *National Geographic*s and hundreds of books and statues and furs and Native American artifacts and various glassware and figurines and wolves' teeth and bear claws and quilts. Beyond the shelves of knickknacks, the back of the store is just as cluttered, with clothes racks and more books, and in the center of it all is a wood-burning stove with a chimney running up to the ceiling. A fire is crackling inside the iron door.

There are two wooden chairs next to the fire, occupied by two old men. They give us a raised hand of acknowledgment and keep on talking. It's not that they're surprised they have customers, but it's clear that getting a sale is not top of mind. This is a way of life. Small-town gossip around the fire in the treasure store. The man on the left has a clean-shaven square jaw and a gigantic bushy white mustache and looks to be in his seventies. He speaks loudly and his tongue has the light lisp of a cartoonish old farmer. The man he is talking to is younger, maybe midfifties or sixty, military-tight hair and tan. They are discussing the younger man's antique Chevy something something. We passed it as we walked in. It is bright green. A car that my friends would drive around LA feeling very cool.

Per usual, I find myself gravitating to the books. I walk up to the wall of old hardcovers. No one has taken a duster to this place in a century. I don't know what I'm looking for. Maybe an old Steinbeck or Emerson. A poetry collection. As my eyes scan, I see a blue-and-green book that I recognize. It's *The Road Unseen,* a book written by my parents. The third and final book in their Walk Across America trilogy. This little book sitting in a small-town store has no idea that the woman who wrote it thirty-five years ago just walked in. Neither do the old men by the fire.

"Mom look at this! It's meant to be!" I hand her the book and she is flushed with tender joy.

She takes it and smiles, turning it over in her hands to inspect that it is real. "Well look at that. I should get it, then." I'm grinning with accomplishment. Finding that book makes me feel like my family has some sort of role in this Oregon country. This beautiful mountain town, so dreamy to me, had my parents' book waiting on its shelves. Somehow, that ties me to this place, for a moment at least, and makes a little case that I belong here. I'm not just a visitor, but a connected piece. The soul at home in the world finds every place remembered.

We go back to fishing through old things. "Should I buy this?" Mom asks, holding up a fur pelt. I touch it and it is impossibly thick fur and very soft. It's a little bigger than a bath mat. She marches over to the two men, who have been ignoring us and talking about someone's wife. "What kind of animal is this?" my mom asks.

"Beaver," the white mustache says.

"How much is it?"

"Ohhhh," he says, making something up, "how's $70?"

"Done," Mom says.

With zero segue, Mom says, "I wrote this book," holding up *The Road Unseen*.

"Is that right?" white mustache says. "Paul Knightly, nice to meet you." He extends his hand from his chair by the fire. We both shake it. "This is my shop," he says with pride.

"We love it," Mom says.

"Ryan Dutton," the other man says with a nod.

Paul slaps his knees. "Wow, a real author in Mount Vernon, what brings you through?"

"My son and I are on a road trip to Florence, Oregon," Mom explains. "His father and I walked across America in the seventies and wrote about it and they were *New York Times* bestsellers, and my son is retracing our steps with me." The words flow out of her. "Jedidiah is a writer like his parents and he's a *New York Times* bestseller too." I blurt a quick laugh and shrug like a twelve-year-old. I've been sifting through a rack of shirts and sweaters to avoid the awkwardness of her speech. In an attempt to swing us back to being customers, I hold up a pink shirt and ask how much it is.

"Oh you want that shirt? That's my shirt," Paul says. "No one ever buys the clothes here. You can have it."

"Oh wow," I say. "Thank you so much." Now he's given me his shirt. We'll be in this store for another hour at least.

"Wow, walked across America," Ryan says, interested but still cool-tempered. The dynamic between the two is pronounced. Ryan is a local, here to gossip and loiter the way small-town people can, without urgency. Paul owns the place. He is a wise elder, sitting by his fire, surrounded by his treasures. He is commanding. Not only does the white mustache say a lot, but he is handsome. Even sitting down, you can tell he is tall.

"A walk across America?" he says. "I think I remember that."

"Well, the books sold over twelve million copies. We started in New Orleans, where I started with his father, and we're headed to Florence. We'll stay in Bend tonight and reach Florence tomorrow."

"I lived in New Orleans once. Years ago. It used to be fun. Very fun. All the bars I went to are gay bars now. I don't care for the male or female gays. But I do love the French Quarter," he says.

I feel a little punch of adrenaline as he says this. Whenever a stranger says something homophobic in front of me, I am flushed, suddenly alert. Not that I'm ready to fight or run, but I'm suddenly listening closely, assessing my safety, I suppose. Usually the comments come when the person thinks they are in the presence of like-mindedness. I can come off as straight. Not to most women, and not to people attuned to cues like diction and innuendo. But country people have often mistaken me for straight. Maybe I'm more performatively masculine in front of them. Maybe my voice drops or I keep my hands down. I can't see myself, so I don't know what things I'm doing unconsciously.

I am also jolted whenever someone brings up homosexuality in front of my mother. I wonder if she will defend me. If she'll challenge this store owner to protect her son.

"Well, a lot of cities have changed so much over the years," she says. "It's not the New Orleans I remember, but the French Quarter is still very beautiful." A small betrayal. I'm not surprised. If she defended me, I would have been shocked.

A couple weeks earlier I had dinner with my dad. He lives in the country, and we went out to a sports bar, the local spot for all the workers at the General Motors plant. After a perfectly forgettable dinner, we were walking back to the car when a man smoking on the patio yelled, "Fuck you faggots!"

I looked over my shoulder and saw a chubby red-faced man, probably my age, smoking a cigarette next to a blond woman. I hadn't been called a faggot in two decades of living in Los Angeles, except for when my gay friends call each other faggots with some reclamation humor. The man yelled it again, louder, "FUCK YOU FAGGOTS!" His tone was not aggressive, but drunk in that masculine playful way that wants to stir shit up to make the other Neanderthals laugh. But there wasn't another pink pig-looking beast with him. Just the woman he was smoking with. "Have a good night!" she yelled at us with a smoker's rasp, an attempt to smooth over the moment. "You too!" I said back with an ironic casual tone.

I wondered if my dad would step in. If he would shout back. He did not. He got in the car. "What were they saying?" he said to me. He might have heard. He might not have. I'm not sure. I assume he didn't, because he is of hot temper. But about this? I don't know. Even now.

"Nothing, they're drunk," I said, moving on from the encounter.

I have learned that I have to protect myself.

Paul continues: "I find things from all over the state, and the world. Lots of Native American things. My wife is Native American; this is her dance cloak," he says, pointing up on the wall to a large leather shawl covered in turquoise beads. "She made that from young leather by hand, for powwows. They have a big pow-wow every year. We also make wine. Did you see the sign that says 'winery' on the door as you came in? That's me."

"We did see that," my mom says in the bright voice of excited curious.

"Would you like to do a tasting?" he asks.

"Oh!" Mom looks at me with a smile, "Want to? I know you're not drinking because of your stomach."

"A tasting is fine. Sounds wonderful," I say.

"OK," Paul says, lifting himself from his recliner by the fire with great effort. He walks over to the counter where his wine bottles are, reaches down for a low shelf, and pulls out some shot glasses and a few bottles of wine with rubber corks on them, already opened.

"First we'll start with a blackberry wine," he says, pouring a splash in a couple of shot glasses. "You get over here, Ryan, I'm pouring you some too." Ryan lumbers over.

"This is from wild picked blackberries in the heart of the Sno-qualmie Valley. It's very unpolluted there. There's a warm aftertaste that lingers on the palate well past sixty seconds. So delicious when served with natural beef or elk stew." He's speaking now as if he's an animatronic character in a museum. The script is re-hearsed. "Also quite complementary with any seasoned pasta. It is medium-sweet. Drink."

I haven't been drinking alcohol, but this is a moment. The energy is heightened. Besides, it's just a tasting. We drink. Mom is flamboyantly pleased with the taste. It is sweeter to me than "medium-sweet." It tastes like fermented candy, but I give him a wide-eyed "mmmmmmm."

"OK, next. Have you ever had honey mead?" He says *mead* with such a heavy *d* that it becomes two syllables. "Mee-duh."

"No, I don't know what that is," Mom says. I shake my head no. "This is the most popular. People order my mead from all over the United States. Do you know where the term *honeymoon* comes from?"

We both say no in unison, like excited kindergartners.

"In medieval times, honey mead was given to the bride and groom after the wedding ritual. They were provided with enough mead to last one full moon. They were supposed to drink it every night and let the good times flow, if you get what I'm saying. Mead was known to promote fertility. They were expected to drink it all over the course of the first month, hopefully ending in a pregnancy. Enough honey mead to last one moon, that's where we get the term *honeymoon*."

"I did not know that!" Mom says, clutching her shot glass close to her chest. Suddenly I'm invisible between them.

"Are you married? Got a boyfriend? Single?" Paul asks.

"No," she says, halting. As if stopping herself from letting the whole story of bad men and marriages spill out.

"You don't have anyone to tell you how pretty your eyes are? That isn't right. My granny taught me if I think something about a woman you ought to tell her. If you lived around here, I'd take you on a date."

"Well," Mom says, looking at me with can-you-believe-it eyes. "That makes my day, thank you so much." Her voice is higher, lighter than normal. A seventeen-year-old girl suddenly inhabiting my mother's body. "Well, I think I need to buy some wine," she grins. "Is this what you say to all the girls to make a sale?"

"No ma'am, I just am an honest man and if I see a beautiful lady, I tell her."

"Well, I'd like a bottle of the blackberry and a bottle of the honey mead, for sure," she says, looking at me, wiggling her shoulders. "We can save this honey mead to have on Christmas, something really special."

We buy the wine and Paul gives us business cards that lead to his very homemade website. It is all so earnest and I'm so glad that we stopped. I feel a pride in our intuition. Our freedom to flip a U-turn and explore, which led us to this man and his mead, a beaver pelt and my mom's book on the shelf, homophobia and flirting. For some people, his derision toward gays would've ruined the experience. And for that, I wouldn't blame them. For me it didn't. I hope that my mom felt a pain for me, even though she stayed quiet. Maybe I should be sad about that. But I'm not. I'm happy she got to flirt. And a cold thought washes through me: that soon, the old people will die off and I won't have to hear comments like that.

We say our goodbyes. Paul and Ryan stand at the door, waving us away like family.

The tiny town disappears, and we are in the country again. Cows and barns and mountain valleys. We have a few more hours to get to Bend and find a hotel.

"Let's listen to the Donner party podcast!" I say with a sinister laugh, ready to jump back into gore.

"I just want to ride quietly for a bit," Mom says.

So we drive through the softening light. We reach Bend in the dark and it feels like a big city. I text my friend Becca, who lives there, for recommendations. She sends us to a brewery that's also a motorcycle garage. We drive straight there. It is very cold. Frigid. The brewery has food trucks outside. We choose a salad truck and get healthy stuff. Mom is kind of quiet. She's in her phone.

I find us a spot to sleep in town, walkable to the main stretch, and we check ourselves in. It is clearly an old motel that has been updated and made superficially cool. The doors are painted bright orange. The lobby has craft beer on tap. The website boasts of a gym, but when I go investigate, it is a closet with two treadmills and fluorescent lights. Dismal. I head back to the room. Mom has washed her face and it is shiny with her oil.

She is on her phone, watching elephants no doubt.

I brush my teeth and crawl into bed. I open the book I brought, Wendell Berry's *The World-Ending Fire,* and barely make it through the first page.

My mom takes off her reading glasses and inhales, as if to ask me something, but pauses.

"Yes?" I say.

"Do you really think he thought I was pretty?"

"Who?"

"The wine man. That old man."

"He seemed like an honest person. You *are* pretty, Mom."

She looks at her phone again. "It feels nice to feel pretty. I haven't heard something like that from a man in a long time."

"Well, not since that European man stalked you in the gas station."

"He really wanted to help me, didn't he?" she says.

"He wanted to marry you."

She puts her reading glasses back on and goes back to her phone, smiling.

Not much later, she is falling asleep to her podcasts, headphones in. I read for a moment longer and decide to sleep. As I turn off the light, I see she has her eyes closed, and she is still smiling.

7

WE WAKE UP EARLY, and I tell Mom I want to get coffee and see the urban riverfront. She is game. We could walk there, but it's too cold, so we drive to a little coffee shop in the old grid of downtown Bend. I ask the barista, "Is there a path along the river?" She scoffs. "Yes, literally behind us, like ten feet that way."

Mom gets a tea because caffeine hurts her joints. I order a big coffee. We walk out into a wall of cold air and wrap around the building to see a park with tall trees and a winding pathway along the river. The paper cup is hot, but my fingers are frozen. The river-walk doesn't border much of a river. They have slowed the Deschutes into a thin, semi-stagnant lake with bridges and trees leaning over. There are geese everywhere and their concomitant shit. The goose-to-shit ratio in any public lake makes geese hardly worth it.

The homes along the river are beautiful and well appointed. It seems like the posh place to live. There are Adirondack chairs sitting in green lawns facing the water and stone-lined firepits and houses with big balconies. The trees are in peak fall colors. It has the feel of what I imagine Japan in the fall is like. A huge willow is orange over the water.

Mom huffs as she bends down to pick a pine cone off the ground. "Boy these pine cones are pretty, wish I had a bag." To do what? Cart them all the way home across the country and put them on a table? They are the most boring pine cones I've ever seen.

Today is the day we will reach Florence, the town on the coast where my parents finished their walk. I kind of forgot. This is the final day. We'll drive from Bend over the mountain pass to Eugene, then on to the coast. About four hours in total. We mosey back to the car and head out.

After Bend, my parents walked over the McKenzie Pass, one of America's coolest roads. It begins on the northeastern side of the Three Sisters mountains, crawling up in elevation from dry and dusty pine trees to an ocean of volcanic rock. The surface of the moon. These mountains block the coastal moisture, and once you pass through the fossilized volcanic mesa, you drop through a wormhole of sorts into thick, neon-green jungle. Then the road winds down the western side in tight switchbacks.

My first time driving it was with my dad on my postcollege motorcycle trip. A man in Bend told us that the route was famous for wrecks. Apparently, not that long ago, a Walmart truck was sent (by an algorithm) up the pass, because it was technically the shortest distance between Bend and Eugene. The truck couldn't make the tight turns and fell off the cliff into the forest. Of course this thrilled me, and Dad and I took the road. Even on a motor-cycle, the switchbacks were hard.

But now Mom and I veer left when we see a huge sign: MCKEN-ZIE PASS CLOSED TO THROUGH TRAFFIC. It's November 8 and the route is closed for the season. We missed it by a week. We end up taking the northern route, Highway 20, which is a larger road that's maintained throughout winter. It is technically longer but less windy and narrow and therefore faster.

It's probably best that McKenzie Pass is closed, because twenty minutes into the new route we drive into a winter storm. The roads are white and the pine trees heavy with pillowy snow. We drive slow, following the tracks made by eighteen-wheelers. It is beautiful. As we cross over the mountains and inch down the other side, the snow changes to icy slush. Then the pine trees are skirted by ferns and the slush turns to rain. We're in the rain forest, just like that.

The microclimates of the West will always amaze the Tennes-sean in me. Between Bend and Eugene, you see three or four en-tirely different worlds. Desert, dry conifer forest, icy volcanic mountaintop, and rain forest. As if the world has been shrunk into an amusement park ride. This is so different from living in Nash-ville. I can drive for six hours in any direction and almost nothing changes. The same types of plants. The same weather. These things I don't understand, but they give me a nice metaphor for travel. If you've never left your bubble, the place that made you, you do not know that what is doesn't have to be. But there are other environ-ments just as real as yours. Other transpositions of reality. Which feels like an invitation of sorts for one's life.

We are now in the Oregon everyone knows. Rainy and green. We pass right through Eugene and head to Florence. I'm now antsy to see it again. And see it with my mom.

I tell Mom that I haven't been to Florence since the first day of my big bicycle trip to Patagonia. I lived on my bicycle for a year and a half, wrote a book about it, and became a writer. My route began in Florence, on the same beach we're visiting today.

"Well, I haven't been there since January of 1979," Mom says, "since the end of our walk."

We're both returning to the site of something that shifted our lives. The end of her great adventure. The beginning of mine.

We follow the windy road along the river that connects Eugene to Florence. Everything is forests and clear-cut used-to-be forests and farms until you plop into town. Florence is not big, and it doesn't seem to be especially anything. It has some hotels and restaurants, but it is neither bougie nor swarming with life. It is sleepy. Perhaps more of a fishing village than a tourist destination. Just south of town, across the Siuslaw River, is the South Jetty RV park and beach. This is where my mom and dad walked across the sand into the Pacific Ocean to finish their walk across America. This is where I carried my bike over the dunes and touched the tires to the water, so that I could begin my journey south.

My mom is glued to the window. She hasn't seen these things in forty-three years.

"It really looks the same," she says. This comforts me.

We park the car in a small lot behind the dunes, the exact parking lot where I clipped into my bike for the first time. I am feeling so many things. The memory of my trip and my mom's nostalgia in the air. She is quiet now, looking out the window, her eyes darting and squinting, as she is working things out. Placing memories and made-up memories, what has changed and what has been lost to forgetting. She doesn't say much. I want her to externally process. I want her to describe everything, remember everything. But she is quiet.

The parking lot is walled off from the ocean by steep dunes and grass, and we have to hike over them. I think Mom can do it, but I'll watch her to see if she needs help.

When we get out of the car, it is windy and cold. But the sun is shining.

I scamper up the dunes. I want to see the ocean, and I want to film my mom. Cresting the dunes, the ocean is loud and roaring. The waves big. Logs litter the beach, smoothed by the tumble of the waves. A man walks with his dog in the distance. It is wild and untouched, no houses or obvious human impact. Just rolling dunes and grass and the churning Pacific. Other than one man walking, the beach is all ours. I turn around and Mom is walking with good speed up the slope. I film her a little. I go back down to get a read on her panting. "Do you need help, Mom? Want my arm?"

"No, I can do it," she says. She is fine. Excited.

She reaches the top of the hill and sees the ocean. Something in me expected her to gaze at the sea and reflect on it with a wise, reclining distance, like Maya Angelou explaining the way things are in God's beautiful plan. A queen gently nodding at her life. But Mom doesn't react like that. She is not kingly. She is childlike. She claps her hands. She chirps, makes quick, high-pitched gasps. "This is it!" she says. She does a little dancing jig, cranking her arms in a circle. Her eyes are full of curiosity at her own life. Not the serene wisdom of "This is how it is," but the youth of "How can this be?"

January 18, 1979. *National Geographic* photographers surrounded her. Hundreds of people from all over America had flown or driven out to walk the last mile with her and Dad. The beach was full of onlookers and excitement. The two of them walked into the water fully clothed, carrying their huge backpacks, and kissed as the cameras snapped. The moment was theirs, and also the world's. Personal history and performance.

"It's sweet that it's just us now," I say.

"Yes honey, it is."

She is smiling and walking slowly, gazing up and down the beach. She looks beautiful, as if her thirty-one-year-old self has risen to the surface of her face. Last time she was here, she was pregnant with my older sister. Now that sister has an eight-year-old daughter. This beach remained, the waves pounding the sand every minute of every month of every year in between. The dunes, the water, disinterested in my mother's life. She is not the main character if you ask the beach.

I wish I could read her mind, or feel her feelings, to know. But I cannot. I am so wrapped up in her moment that I forget this is my moment, too. Right now, I am not interested in myself. I'm interested in her.

We walk down to the water. "Mom, you have to touch it!"

"I do, don't I?" she asks, her voice distracted.

She walks to the edge of where the waves are licking the sand, and a bigger wave sends the water reaching farther and faster than she can move away. Her shoes get wet. She is laughing. I wish we would jump in the surf. There is something about the fullness of submerging in water, of letting the wave wash over you, that cements the moment. Baptism has always made sense to me. Submerging oneself and returning wet is excellent symbolism for rebirth.

We don't hug. I don't notice at the time, but later, as I'm writing, I do. Instead, we walk up the beach, the roar of the waves making it hard to talk. Mom bends down every ten feet to pick something up. We continue for a while, letting the achievement of our arrival really settle; then, in the smallest moment, the turning of a thought, the notion of "we've walked far enough down this beach, let's turn around" dawns on us, and the trip changes course. We transition from going to returning. Like the winter solstice, there is a moment where the whole earth shifts, the planet turning its North Pole back toward the sun. We cannot feel this, but many of the biggest changes—in nature, in life—go unnoticed. They happen without the moment ever being named.

My mom lets out a sigh of completion. "Yeah, I'm ready," she says, and we turn around. As we walk I see that she has collected some shells. Broken and ugly shells. Of course she has.

"I'll put these in a jar," she says, looking at them.

We climb back over the dune and down to the parking lot. We kick sand off our shoes and plop into the car. I let out a big exhale to jump-start a conversation. "We did it. What was it like, being back there?"

"It was beautiful. Just like I remember it," she says.

"How do you feel?"

"I feel good. I can't believe I walked all the way from New Orleans to here."

I nod, dissatisfied. I want her to give me an Oprah speech. A commencement address about memory, hardship, and dreams deferred and replaced. But she has her hands folded in her lap, looking out the window.

"I can't believe it either," I say, and start the car.

"Let's go to some thrift stores in town," Mom says as we drive.

"OK, great. I really want to find a sweatshirt or hat that says Florence, Oregon, on it."

"There was a hotel somewhere that your dad and I stayed in, and they threw us a big dinner and party, for a hundred plus people. But it should be right around here by this bridge and I don't see it."

"Well, it's been over forty years. It could've been torn down in the eighties."

"That's true," she says, still looking.

Come on, say more! I take a moment to interrogate my expectations. What do I want from her? I want understanding. I want to see that she has grown wise and poetic from life. I want her to analyze and reflect. It may be a generational difference. Millennials are comfortable with therapy, with unpacking trauma, with healing the inner child and talking about foundational wounds. We were raised on all of that. Baby boomers are tougher. Constant analysis was not modeled for them. And to look too closely might open a wound long calloused. Smile and keep going. *Keep calm and carry on.*

I want to talk and talk until there are no more words and the feelings are splayed out like a pig roast on a spit. She doesn't have words for me right now.

We've seen the elephant. And I am unsatisfied. I wouldn't say it was a disappointment, but it wasn't fireworks. It was simple, a mother and a son walking on a beach that could've been anywhere.

We arrive at the thrift store and the clothes are dismal. Nothing but boxy, bad flannels and cardboard-thick T-shirts. But at the back wall, behind the shelves of vases and mismatched cups and spoons, is a wall of CDs. It runs from floor to ceiling, an incredible collection that must number in the thousands. Many of the CDs are still in their plastic. An old store must have gone out of business and brought their inventory here. The collection is alphabetized, and my eyes fall on *C.* Celine Dion. They have four or five copies of *Let's Talk About Love,* her album from 1997. It has the Titanic song on it. One of the cases is open, so I take out the booklet, fading and frayed. Immediately I am deluged with memories. I bought that CD the year it came out. I was fourteen and nothing unlocked my gayness like Celine Dion. In my room I had one of those boom boxes with detachable speakers and a tray that slid out with slots for six CDs. I put Celine in there, detached the speakers, and stuck them on either side of my head, pointed inward. I submerged myself in the sound of Celine's voice, the orchestra behind her, the Titanic flute. I would rewind her runs and obsess over her vocal choices.

Around that time, my mom took me to see her in concert. I don't know how she afforded it, but we were in the second row. I sang along to "All by Myself," "It's All Coming Back to Me Now," all of the hits. I hit my chest with my hand the way Celine did. I lost myself completely, not yet old enough to be embarrassed by my femininity, or to realize that loving Celine Dion was a tell. I loved what I loved. I had Matt Damon's face hanging in my room. A *Vanity Fair* cover of him in the bathtub with a toothbrush hanging out of his mouth. I was obsessed. I said I loved his acting, and I really thought that was it. I remember asking Mom, "Why do you think I love Matt Damon so much?" genuinely looking for an answer. I didn't register the comedy of this. I just wanted to talk about this man who consumed my thoughts. Talking about him made him feel closer. "Well, honey," she said, "you are artistic, and he is a fabulous actor. You recognize talent."

I wonder now what my mom thought of all of this, watching her teenage son clutch his chest, singing Celine songs and rocking back and forth.

I hold the CD in my hand and turn it over. I haven't thought about this album in decades, and if you'd asked me, I couldn't have recalled it from memory. But holding it, my brain recognizes every detail—the font choices, the track listing—pulling them out from a filing cabinet in the basement of my brain. Seeing it in person unlocked it all.

I decide I'm buying it. My eyes scroll across the wall of nostalgia looking for other albums. Whoa. Sarah McLachlan, *Fumbling Towards Ecstasy*. I remember my seventh-grade science teacher Miss Swan playing that album over and over at science camp as I washed dishes in the cafeteria with her. A few rows over, there's the Postal Service. I remember listening to that on my drives to and from Hermosa Beach in college. Sheryl Crow, *Tuesday Night Music Club*. Windows down in my first car, with a portable CD player plugged into a tape adapter. Each album initiates a rush of feelings.

A thought arrives, uninvited: my youth was a generation ago. These are oldies. I don't even own a CD player anymore.

I buy all four albums for a dollar each. Mom has found a denim shirt with embroidered cats on it. She models it for me, giving a little spin. "This is hand-done! The boomers are going to be so jealous."

We make our purchases, get back in the car, and begin driving east.

We've done it. We've seen the ocean. It's a beeline for Nashville now. We'll make it back to Bend tonight.

"Let's give a cult a try," Mom says, opening her podcast app.

"Ooh, reptilians and aliens and the end times, the cult of Sherry Shriner, wanna listen to that?"

"Whoa, yes. I've heard of people believing in reptilians taking over the world, but I don't really know much about it."

"Done," she says, hitting Play as we drive toward the Cascades.

The story starts with a murder, or a suicide. It's a little hard to classify what happened. The police arrived at Steven Mineo's apartment and found him dead. Shot in the head by his girlfriend Barbara Rogers. But the 911 call and her subsequent trial muddy the waters. "My boyfriend had a gun," Rogers said. "He told me to hold it here and press the trigger." Apparently he wanted to die. They were drunk and high and he had been rejected by his guru, his spiritual leader Sherry Shriner. He fell into depression. And he had a gun. He handed it to Barbara, pulled it close and pressed it on his forehead, and begged her to pull the trigger. She was crying and protesting. He kept pleading for it. Finally she did it. His head exploded and his body slumped to the floor. And Barbara called 911 in hysterics.

Who is Sherry Shriner, and why did she have such power over Steven Mineo?

"Ooh my," Mom says, adjusting her weight to sit at attention.

Sherry Shriner's voice comes on. She sounds like she swallows cigarettes whole, and she has a lot to say. Big theories about how the world works.

Shriner's ideas originally gained her a following on Facebook. Then she started a radio show, where she'd talk for hours and hours about the elite cabal of aliens that rules the world. Specifically, reptilians. She called herself a "Messenger of the Highest God," and her worldview went something like this: There is a New World Order, where everyone from Barack Obama and Joe Biden to Mariah Carey and Tom Hanks and the Queen of England are all aliens in disguise, ruling over us in an attempt to subjugate and destroy the human race. They want to establish one overarching world government. "We've been seeing it on a massive scale," she explained in one radio show. "Celebrities, news announcers, even people in commercials. Everyone you see on TV, about 90 percent, is a clone or a synthetic robotoid."

In her videos and radio show, Sherry would drone on and on about who was a clone, who was a reptilian, and when the world would end. Which always seemed to be imminently. Her YouTube channel had more than twenty thousand followers.

Barbara Rogers and Steven Mineo were deep into Sherry Shriner's philosophies. She kept her followers in line through her hyperactivity on Facebook. It was a common thing for her to turn on someone, call out one of her followers for being compromised and perhaps even a reptilian. When she turned on you, you were out.

A few years after getting into the world of Sherry Shriner, Barbara Rogers posted on her Facebook that she liked eating raw meat. Yes, that is a little weird, but Sherry Shriner saw it and replied, "There's only certain types of people who crave the raw meat, because they crave blood . . . those with the vampire demon in them."

"Facebook will end civilization," I say to Mom.
"I like Facebook," she says.

Mineo's discipleship unraveled once he saw Shriner turn on his girlfriend—someone he knew to be real. He became convinced she was a fraud and dedicated himself to exposing her. He uploaded five videos in the spring and summer of 2017, pleading with people to see her as the liar she was. Shriner went on the defensive and labeled Rogers a "Vampire Witch Reptilian Super Soldier!"

Sherry never met Steven Mineo or Barbara Rogers in person. She led her ministry almost entirely from behind her computer in rural Ohio. In that way, she was a precursor to QAnon. On Facebook, her profile picture was an image of the White House at night with a green alien head floating above it. She never posted photos of herself and never filmed videos of herself talking. If you go deep enough into Google, the only photo of her looks to be from the mideighties. Her hair is blond and fluffy, like she sings for Journey. She looks to be young, in her twenties or early thirties. She has a slight smirk, like she knows a secret.

After Mineo's death, Sherry called the entire incident a PSYOP against her. She claimed on Facebook and her radio show that she was trying to protect Steve from Barb by exposing Barb as a reptilian. "He was very upset that she killed him," Sherry said, describing a vision God sent her of the whole situation. "I'll be very frank," he said. "That bitch killed me."

I'm listening to this and thinking of Christianity. Of all the times a youth pastor or friend said they had a "word" from the Lord, and how definitive that was. A conversation killer, a block to any challenge. One of my college friends dated every hot Christian girl on campus and broke up with them after a month because "God is leading my heart away." *Oh, is He?* I remember thinking. *Or are you just horny and hot and blaming God for your libido?*

This podcast has me in my thoughts. I'm listening to Sherry blacklist people by calling them reptilians. She can just decide who is in the club and who isn't. Evangelicals used a version of this tactic on me in my twenties. They told me that my sexuality was caused by "opening myself up to demons" and "allowing the great Deceiver in." They could discount anything by calling it demonic. They weaponized the unseen spiritual realm to fit a narrative they were handing down to the next generation.

This is why I have such a visceral reaction to the spiritual. To crystals and tarot cards and readings and the proclamations of empaths and healers. I'm certain much of it is positive and helpful, but it reminds me too much of the people who sanctioned their thoughts as Godly "downloads" during the most vulnerable years of my life. How much of the world's insanity is perpetrated by people claiming to have a direct connection to God?

Mom is listening intently as Sherry talks about the sources she's studied, from the Bible to the Gnostic Gospels to Aztec prophecies. When she mentions the non-biblical sources, Mom chimes in, "See right there, that's where she let the Devil in."

8

WE PULL INTO BEND, OREGON, and find a dingier hotel than the last one. But it'll do. Hotels feel more transactional by this point. Everything is less interesting now that we've achieved the ultimate destination.

We sleep fast and wake up early, thinking we'll hit Wyoming tonight.

We listen to quiet music and make excellent time. I realize we've got only a few days of driving left. And I haven't asked my mom the question. The one I've been avoiding because reaching the Pacific Ocean has filled the top spot of my thoughts. But now the trip is nearing an end. I am squeezed for time, a feeling I so often feel. I can procrastinate no longer.

"You know, we never talked about it, I'm so curious," I say, grinding my hands on the leather steering wheel. I am looking ahead at a straight road and barren land, as if the earth has cleared itself to give space for this conversation. "I remember when I sent you those bombshell emails just about my perspective on faith and sexuality. They were really long, you remember?"

"Yes," Mom says, calmly and matter of fact. Her voice is gentle, but betraying a controlled alertness.

"You wrote back, 'You've given me a lot to think about.'"

"I remember that," she says.

"Well, I think one of the biggest things, truly the final holy grail of my life journey of understanding, is the idea of when and if I ever fall in love and get married, to a man. . . . I've always wondered, would my mom come to the wedding? I wouldn't want her to come reluctantly. It's supposed to be the happiest day of my life, so any negative energy or even complex energy would ruin the day. I would only be worried about you instead of what I'm experiencing."

The words keep tumbling out. I'm speaking in staccato short sentences, constantly revising my phrases to find the right words. Trying to soften the conversation and be clear.

"Because that day will come," I continue after a half second of quiet. "No question. And if you are like, 'I'm not comfortable,' then, I mean, I've been planning for over a decade to not have you there. And that's fine. It really is. I have completely compartmentalized my life. That's fine. There's lots of parts to life. You go to Republican rallies, and I don't need to hear all about it. You know what I'm saying? But . . . would you come, would you want to come? Or would you feel too conflicted and feel like you're endorsing something that you don't believe in?"

The air is thick. My ears throb as if they have water in them.

"Well Jed," she shifts her weight. She fixes her hair and puts her hands on her knees. She is not looking at me. She is looking at the road ahead. "Your journey is your life and your decisions. And . . . you're asking me to understand things that I don't. And to accept things that truly go against my core beliefs. And that has nothing to do with how much I love you. You're bone of my bones and flesh of my flesh. But I do not understand homosexuality, and . . ." She searches for words. "There's nothing that you could do that would stop my love for you."

"And I truly know that."

"As your mother, I pray for you and I put you in the Lord's hands, because it is your life, it's not mine. It's your life. And—" She is quiet, thinking, with a long pause of silence.

I jump in, bulldozing my stress with words. "I try to find, like, a metaphor where I can understand that perspective, because it's not like a political belief. I understand that good, sane people can disagree about politics and religion. If you were like, 'Jed, can you accompany me to this Republican Convention? I have no one to go with,' I could be like, 'OK, well, I don't agree with a lot of the policies. Deeply. But OK, if it means a lot to you.' But, if you said, 'I want to go to Sherry Shriner's convention,' I would say, 'That's too dangerous in my opinion, and I love you, but I can't do that.' And if you were like, 'This is core to who I am,' to believe in her, I'd be like, 'OK, well, you do that, and I'll love you when I can, but I can't do that part.' And . . . I guess the difference for me is that, like, well, I don't know what the difference is. There are pillars of what a child wants from their parent, which are to be loved, to be liked, and to be approved of."

Mom tilts her head, considering these three things.

"And I know I've got the first two in spades," I continue. "And I may never get the last one. And that's fine. But I'll always want it. It truly is, I think, the final piece of my sense of adulthood. It's the only thing that has any power over me. That desire for approval. But I, I do believe in the power and structure of a committed relationship in the sense where, when I do build my life with someone, that will come first. And if they're uncomfortable around you, I, I'll choose them. Not that I won't come see you and still maintain a wonderful friendship with you. And it just seems like such a shame that, in my opinion, something that is not necessarily connected to the gospel in any way—and, I think, just, culturally antiquated—could be such a major sticking point."

"We've both heard all the arguments, pro and con," she says. "But for me, it goes against nature. Biologically. God created a man and a woman."

Here we go again. Saying what we believe and where our beliefs diverge, throwing words at brick walls. I know I can't win her with argument, any more than she can win me. So why try? But I try.

"So, what is it when someone is born intersex and they're neither male or female? They have both genitals? What is that? That's natural. What does God want from that person? I don't think they're an abomination, they just are." I catch myself speaking like I'm in a college debate class. I'm arguing on Twitter with an American flag avatar. My mother is sitting right there next to me, and we are talking about the unspeakable. The thing I fear most.

"What's amazing about being an adult is that I really do not feel a charge in this conversation like I would have ten years ago," I say. "Because I know that you love me and I really respect boundaries, and I understand that people have deep beliefs that are different. But I am really trying as I approach forty to be in a place where no conversations frighten me."

"They shouldn't," she says.

"Some conversations can be uncomfortable, but— Look at that rain," I say and point out the window at storm clouds dumping in a vast field.

The car is quiet for a moment. I want her to speak.

"I've always wanted for you Jed, in the deepest part of you, to love and be loved, but with a woman, not a man. And there are many things in life as you get older that you accept the fact that you don't understand. There are many things in life that you just literally have to turn over and put in the hands of God. Because it's either too complex or too difficult. All kinds of things. But, I think the life that homosexuals live is, um, is just more difficult."

"Why?" I ask, sharp and fast.

"Well, first of all, they can't procreate."

"Lots of heterosexual people can't procreate."

"Heterosexual people are male and female."

"I know, but lots of them are sterile or infertile."

Pause.

She takes a big breath.

"You're a very intelligent man. In your mind, you've worked out all the answers. And all the reasons you want to live a homosexual life. There's no argument, there's no other point of view that is going to break through."

I am seized cold in my heart. The little boy in me is curled up and invisible. The robot of my mind is driving. I am thinking clearly, like a computer.

"Well, yeah," I say, "I'm afflicted with something that's caused me incredible hardship that I don't want. And I've spent my life studying it to try to understand. And it's poked incredible holes in the traditional evangelical understanding of it, that to me are irreversible. And it does intrigue me, as someone who lives with this, and you do not live with it, nor do you understand it, that you wouldn't trust my experience. And you would trust the experience or opinions of lots of other people who haven't experienced it."

"No parent would wish or want their child to be a homosexual, Jed." She's looking at me now. "No parent."

"That's not true. I know a lot of parents that are praying that their kids are gay. It's only a hard life for a child because of the lack of acceptance. The only negative thing is cultural oppression. But once you get out of that mindset . . . once you live in a culture of acceptance, it's completely normal to be gay. It's wonderful. But anyway, we don't have to go deep into the justifications of homosexuality." I feel a fatigue relitigating those emails. I know that isn't how to win. And so does she. "I just wanted to ask you about my wedding day. Because that day will come, and I don't want to assume something and then hurt your feelings."

A long beat in silence.

"My prayer has always been that something, whatever the key is, that something would turn your heart and interest to women," Mom says with a pleading tenderness.

"Mine, too. And I sent a girl to therapy over it, trying to date her. I traumatized her because she felt like I was experimenting on her."

What feels like minutes pass in silence. We've reached that place in every impassable argument where we are just repeating our same positions with slightly different words. We're in the death spiral of planted feet.

"So how do you envision your life, Jed?" she asks.

"The rest of my life?"

"Yes."

"Mmm . . . I'm very open to whatever God brings me, but I would like a husband and maybe two or three adopted kids. And I'll just be a writer . . . and if kids are not in the cards, then I'll just be a really great uncle and, you know, a resource of love for people. If a great partner comes around, which I hope he does, then I'll build a life with him. I know several incredible gay and lesbian couples. They've been together ten, twenty years. And I'm just like, that's great."

We are quiet again. Mom is thinking. My face is tingling. As calm as I think I feel, my body is a furnace.

"You know, it's very interesting, our very core beliefs. And is there a lie in a core belief?" she says.

"What do you mean?"

"Well, homosexuality, either God created it or he didn't. Either God approves of it or He doesn't. Either it is or it isn't a sin."

"I know you know the Bible so well, but the Bible also outlaws certain things like lending money for interest or divorce unless it's adultery. And then culture says, 'Well, if he hits you, you can divorce him.' And it's like, OK, well, that's not what the Bible said, so someone made a choice. And is God furious with that person, or is God like, 'I gave you these guidelines in a culturally specific moment. And it's the spirit of the law, not the letter of the law.' I don't know . . . I mean, I'm sincerely asking you—"

"Yeah, mmmm," she nods her head in agreement, listening and thinking.

"I mean, I think your question implies that God is a way that he might not be. Which is, either something is right or wrong. Period. If that's true, then, you know . . . doesn't the Church of Christ denomination believe that if you're not Church of Christ, you're not a real Christian?"

"Yes. Well, they believe, and a lot of sects believe that. 'If you don't belong to mine, then you're not gonna get to heaven.'"

"Right? And it's just like, maybe that's true, or maybe that's a really small-minded way of seeing God."

"Well I can certainly speak from life after having been divorced, and understanding why God hates divorce and the Bible says He hates divorce, because of, not only the pain and the ripping, but the damage it does to everybody involved, and particularly the children. So. When scripture talks about God doesn't approve of this or that, there's usually a reason."

"Totally, I agree," I say.

"And a lot of things we don't understand until we do it and we see it really doesn't work."

"Right. Are you saying divorce doesn't work?" I ask.

"No, what I'm saying is that a lot of people think, 'Oh well, divorce, it's not a big deal. You know, if it doesn't work out, we'll just get divorced.' And they don't understand that there is lifelong fallout. And just as you know people who have had successful homosexual relationships, there are equally as many, maybe more, who have had terrible experiences and who want to get out of that lifestyle."

"Well, the same could be said for straight marriages. Most marriages end in divorce in this country. I don't want what a lot of straight marriages are."

Another long beat of silence. The storm is passing far to the south. The land is still empty. Even the other cars seem to be quieter for us.

"Well I think sometimes you have to listen, because there is such a thing as a conviction of the Holy Spirit."

"Right," I say, pulling on my ear. "I don't believe that. Well, maybe I do. Because I'm very convinced that your stance on homosexuality is wrong, and I can say that it is the Holy Spirit telling me this. I tried for fifteen years to believe your position. And it felt like acid in my veins, and I went to that conversion therapy place, and it was the most dark thing I've ever been to. It was sad. And I'm like, this is not life and life abundant, this is not the fruit of the Spirit—"

I stop myself from flying into my rote defenses. *Zoom out, Jed.*

"But anyway, I think that's the profundity and the importance of the nature of our relationship. I mean, this is such a core belief to me, and most gay people, that most people wouldn't be able to have a relationship with their mother over this. And I know many that don't. And I don't know what it is about us. I mean, it's love, and it's also friendship. It's also boundaries, I guess."

"You will notice I have never ridiculed you," she says. "My position is, Jed, that this is bigger than me, it's bigger than you. My position has always been, 'God, I put Jed in your hands,' and my prayer will continue to be, 'Lord, however he is wired, wire him where he's interested in women and not men. Where he's attracted physically and sexually to women, and not men.' I can't fix you, change you, I can't do anything but put you in the hands of God."

"Right, mmm," I pause to think. "And that prayer has been profoundly wounding to me my whole life."

We're quiet. The hum of the car seems loud now.

"And why has it been wounding?" she asks.

"Because who you love is so ingrained and deep, and . . . I mean, if I prayed every day for you to be in love with women, and you said, 'That will never happen.' And I'm like, 'Well, I pray every day,' that would probably bother you, wouldn't it? Your prayers won't work because that is not what God wants. I tried to like women. And it's just not there, any more than it would be for you. And so, your belief that my pursuit of love and relationship and connection is rooted in either a lie or a demonic spirit in me . . . is so poisonous. To know that your mother thinks that about you while you're pursuing something that you find to be beautiful and life giving—it's just a horrible thing to think about."

"Well again," she says sweetly and light, to lower the temperature, "there are a lot of things that words cannot convey, and the Bible talks about. 'Praying in the spirit,' because you don't even know how to pray because it's beyond your mind, it's beyond your conception. When I say I'm praying for you Jed, put aside all the things you believe about homosexuality and all the justifications and this and that . . . I just say, 'God, I'm looking at your word, your word says this, but here is my son, who has this struggle in his life. It's not what I would've chosen for his life.' "

"It's only a struggle because of you. In no other part of my life is it a struggle."

Mom drops her head. Considering and thinking. "Well. Then maybe I'm the last holdout for another ray of truth to come into your mind."

The rain is still off in the distance. I don't know how much time has passed in this conversation. Five minutes? An hour? The world looks like we haven't moved. No exits on the highway. No trees. Just the flat earth and us.

"I can look back in my life and see where I was deceived about a lot of things because I wanted to believe something," she says. "And there's just almost a veil of deception in the world, whether it's marriage, divorce, whatever, and I think homosexuality, and I am not denying your feelings or attractions or anything like that, but I think it is a spiritual deception, and I do not think that God's purpose is for a man and a man or woman and a woman to be together."

I nod my head. "Yeah." We drive in more silence. I'm tired.

"I think from my point of view, as a mother, it hurts deeply that . . . I'm not judging or faulting you for your feelings, but it hurts me deeply that you would choose that kind of lifestyle. Because . . . you may not think it is abnormal, but it is."

Now I want this conversation to stop.

"It really isn't abnormal," I say. "But yeah, I chose it. Well, I didn't choose it, I woke up with it and then I chose to not be that way for my entire youth. And tried conversion therapy, tried speaking in tongues, tried prayers, studied the Bible every day, the prayer closet, sobbed, dated girls. And living that lie was drinking poison. And I don't think that's what God wants for me. I don't understand why God would give us a heart and experiences, if following him felt like deep spiritual dishonesty every day."

"And that is your experience Jed, which I am not denying. But I don't understand it. I mean, Jesus said, I came to give you a life to give it to you more abundantly. Not to beat you over the head with a hammer every day of your life and make you feel like you're a pile of dung."

"Yeah, that's the crux of my point. When Jesus says, 'You will know good teaching by its fruit' and 'I come to give you life, and life abundant,' that is the lens through which you read women speaking in church."

"But that has nothing to do with sexuality."

"Absolutely, it does."

"It has nothing to do with being male and female."

"I absolutely believe it does. I mean, you've long since decided that this is an abomination, even though you don't understand it and you've never experienced it. And I'm not going to change your mind. Only God can do that. And I know you feel the same about me. And maybe you don't believe how sincere I was in my journey to being straight, but it was very sincere. And if the Holy Spirit is real, I have to believe that it confirms when you move toward it and it rebukes when you move away from it. And all I felt in my twenties, when I pursued your prayer for me, was rebuke and pain. The way that you talk about Sherry Shriner, like, 'There's no love in her heart,' and the way that I felt the vitriol and the venom of the Christian community in the name of love, of me being healed. I really do believe they thought they were doing the right thing, but there was just not life in their eyes, there was just not truth in their eyes."

"At the end of the day, it really is your life and your journey and your walk with God."

"Well, exactly."

Mom takes a big inhale. "As I've grown older, I've found that my walk with the Lord has grown sweeter and sweeter. When I say to you, Jed, 'I don't understand your life experience,' it hurts me because I can't help you, I can't change you, I can't make everything idyllic. But I know that the living God that I serve, he has a plan and a purpose for you. And I believe, my prayer for you, is that as you grow older, as intelligent as you are, as many books as you read, that you would just read the scripture. Not because I want you to be this way or that way. Just for your own walk with God. You've been putting yourself as the decision maker. As a follower of Christ, you humble yourself and say, Lord, I don't know."

"Totally. And what I'm saying is, I don't know, but I've tried. And the only thing that feels true is this route, and the other route feels false. And so if I'm wrong . . . then God either has blinded me like he did Pharaoh, which is cruel, or I'm right."

"But it's not about you being right, or me being right. It's about following the Lord and doing His will, not your will, not my will. I mean Jesus, even to the cross, said, 'Father, not my will but thy will be done.'"

"OK, OK, right. Right. I just . . . wanted to make sure I knew your position. And I love you, and I know you love me and I know you like me, and respect me, as I respect you."

We sit in silence for a long time. I am all feeling and no thoughts. I feel sad and somehow relieved. Relieved that I know her answer, that the amorphous wondering is clear.

My mom is just as strong in her position as she ever was. She is convinced. I am convinced. I hoped that the emails had softened her, and maybe, just maybe, she'd changed her mind. She had not. But I am comforted by the fact that she knows she cannot understand. And I am mad that her lack of understanding doesn't cause her to trust me. No, she trusts what the Bible says, the same book that takes slavery for granted and endorses women's silence in church.

She will not change her mind about my sexuality, about homosexuality, about who I love. The Bible is clear. These are not malleable beliefs. For some reason, for her, they are foundational. And I have to decide, does my mother's believing these things disqualify her from a relationship with me? Can I love and enjoy a person who, at her core, believes my "lifestyle" is against God?

Something like an exhale happens inside me as we drive in the silence. *I will never win this argument. She will never change. You've been waiting, hoping for change, and that hope has kept you paralyzed in the imagined moment: What if she embraces and endorses all, or what if she says she doesn't? Two universes split depending on the outcome. And she, too, has been waiting, praying, and hoping for change. For you to turn to the Lord and reject your beliefs. How could you? It would be a betrayal of the obvious truth. And she would say the same for herself.*

Now, without hope, you are free.

The air in the car is water-thick. The cracks in the interstate make loud thuds as we drive. Every sound is amplified.

I let out a big, happy-sounding sigh. Some symbol of moving on.

"Let's get back to the cults!" I say. "Should we try another cult?" I need to exit the silence, need to cheer her up, unable to bear her quietness.

"Oh yes," she says, performing excitement but weighted by the loss of amiability. She sounds beat down and it hurts my heart. There is something in me that wants to see her strong, even if it's belligerent against me. I want to protect her in this moment. I want to live the lie of conversion therapy and forced straightness or celibacy to make her OK.

"Let's go back to Sherry Shriner," I say. I look up her name and find a whole season of episodes. We hit Play.

In 2016 Sherry self-published a book called *Interview with the Devil*. She described herself like this: "I Sherry Shriner, an angel in the flesh, an angel from the past, a queen even, known as queen Shazerazi in heaven, on earth I'm just a humble grandmother, mother and servant of the most high who figured out a way with some help to kick Lucifer's butt."

She sold a product called orgonite, a melted-together combination of crystals and metal set in a resin mold. Sometimes shaped like a pyramid, or a disk. It was supposed to harness energy, repel demons, crash UFOs, and dissolve chemtrails right out of the sky. Shriner made it central to her ministry and sold it on her website.

"I have an orgone necklace," Mom says. "It's not just cuckoo Sherry. Lots of people use orgone for protection."

"Of course you have a necklace," I laugh.

"Can never be too protected."

It's getting dark and I start looking for a diner or restaurant. I find a spot on the main street in Laramie, Wyoming. It's got the look of an old saloon, with a pressed-tin roof and a big bar at the back. The décor is almost good, but ruined by a few bad choices. A string of neon lights runs underneath the bar, casting a green glow on the floor like a hovering UFO. There is some local art on the wall, clearly made by the worst artist alive. It's an acrylic painting of a woman with long flowing hair jumping through the air. They are selling it for $300. Interior design in a small town is almost always nuts, skewed by something. Why this is, I don't exactly know. I would've assumed it came from isolation. But we live in the age of Pinterest and Instagram. Inspiration is everywhere and easily accessible.

We sit down and a young girl comes to serve us.

"Should we have some wine?" Mom asks, perky and ready to be happy again. I haven't had a whole drink in days. But today's conversation makes me want the release. "Absolutely," I say.

"Ooh, this place looks so delicious! Great work finding this!" She holds the big laminated menu up to her face.

"God bless Google," I say, reviewing the menu. I order a steak salad. Mom orders a Caesar salad and two glasses of red wine as she looks at me with a grin. The wine arrives quickly.

Mom holds up her cup. "Cheers!" she says, and leans forward onto the table, giving me eye contact. "I want you to know I approve of you, Jed, I do approve of you," she says, with a mix of playfulness and sincerity. "That doesn't mean I endorse a same sex or adulterous lifestyle," she says through a big smile, "but I approve of you with all my heart."

I smile and clink my glass to hers. "Cheers, Mom. I love you."

"I love you more," she says and sips her wine. "You know, I learned this a long time ago, with your father, and men, and just, through my life . . . but it's a fundamental question. Would you rather be right, or happy?"

I'm not sure what she means, but it means something. She approves of me, with a "but." She doesn't "endorse." We have different definitions of words. Per usual. In spite of this, I don't dissect or press. I smile and allow myself to feel warm.

After a bit of a silence, she asks, "How's your health been today? Feeling any of the pain?"

"I think I'm totally better. I haven't felt that in a few days."

"Connect the dots, Jed! Prayer. Colloidal silver. Vitamins. Momma's love."

"Oh I connect the dots," I say rolling my eyes. "Maybe it just healed with time. Or maybe inhaling tiny metal particles went into my bloodstream and killed any impurities."

"Exactly!" she says.

Another roadside hotel. Another night of Mom cuddling up in her bed with elephant videos. We're driving big ten-hour days. We've seen the Pacific Ocean and we want to be home.

The route to Nashville is I-80 to I-29, which runs down to Kansas City, then across I-70 to St. Louis, then down into western Kentucky and into Tennessee. We can do it in two long days.

The driving is quieter, heavier than it was before. Everything feels colored by the big conversation. Like getting news of a death on vacation. But this isn't the first time we've had a blowout, and it probably won't be the last. Or will it? This really is my final question. But no, it can't be. There will come a day when I introduce my mom to my partner. A day when he's invited or not invited on a family trip, and that means I go or don't go. We've gone over this, my mom and me. I told her that I would choose my husband over her, and if she doesn't get it together, that day is coming. The day when I don't spend holidays with her anymore because I don't feel comfortable bringing my man to her house. I gave her these ultimatums, *Agree with me or see me less,* in hopes of getting her to change. But it doesn't work. Because she is operating on a timeline of prayer and God's will. If she keeps praying, the day that I bring a man home may never come. God will answer her prayer. And here I am, thirty-eight, and I still haven't brought a man home. She's seventy-four years old. Her prayers have kept him away this long. So why not keep praying? Why give in now?

I would argue that her prayers aren't the thing that's kept him away. It's the decades of unpacking I've had to do, just to get to the baseline where I can have a romantic relationship. It's the fear of rejection that I carried through my teens and twenties. Is it that prayer works or that religious trauma stunts a life?

As we drive into the Great Plains, I put on a podcast about the 1619 Project and critical race theory's history. Normally I would never play such a thing with her in the car, but I am tired. I want to smoke cigarettes in front of her. I want to listen to liberal podcasters raging against Trump supporters. I want to be myself, al-most as punishment.

The podcast begins, explaining the new wave of book bans in schools and the panic around white kids feeling guilty about their skin color. Mom is reading something on her phone. She speaks up over the audio:

"Do you know the origin of the word *riffraff*?"

I turn down the radio. "No, I do not."

"Well, it comes from medieval French." She begins reading loudly over the podcast. "There was an expression, *rifle et rafle*. . . . *Rifle*, 'to spoil or strip,' and *rafle*, 'to carry off' . . . and it sort of meant everyone and everything, but over time came to be known as the bottom of society." She looks at me over her reading glasses. "How interesting is that! OK, now how about this, the phrase *a shot of whiskey*?"

"No I don't know." The podcast drones quietly in the back-ground. I cannot understand what they're saying.

"In the old west, a .45 cartridge for a six-gun cost twelve cents. So did a glass of whiskey. If a cowhand was low on cash he would often give the bartender a cartridge in exchange for a drink. This became known as a 'shot' of whiskey."

"Wow that's so interesting. Where are you reading that?"

"Some website!"

I turn the podcast off.

"You know, Dandy loved things like this," she says. "Old say-ings and old words." She's smiling at the memory. Dandy was one of my mom's best friends when I was a child. Her name was Mar-tha Belle, but my siblings and I called her Dandy because that's what her grandkids called her. She was a mentor of sorts to my mother, a sounding board, the type of friend who teaches you the way of the world. She lived in a big antebellum mansion near our farm. I remember our family station wagon turning onto her long driveway, how it felt to see her standing on the porch, curly gray hair, tall and regal. I loved her. My mom loved her.

Years ago, my mom wrote a book about the profound women in her life, and Dandy had a chapter. She told the story of Dandy losing her husband to a heart attack, getting her real estate license at sixty, and starting her life over.

> I asked her if she thought she had a future, even at her age. She was over 60 and I didn't want to offend her.
>
> "Oh, ma stars. Bawbra! Ya can start a new life at 50, 60, or 85. Yaw life is just beginnin'. Why you can start a new life at 90!" She threw her head back and laughed. "Just give me a chance!"

"I remember Dandy so well," I say, turning to Mom as I drive. "As a kid, I mean. But I don't really know what happened to her. Didn't she move to Memphis?"

"It's a sad story. When Martha was around seventy, she sold her farm and moved to Memphis to be near her daughters. A couple years later, she married an older gentleman she met at her church. I rarely saw her afterwards. Her new husband was a retired oil executive, a widower and very possessive, controlling and demanding. He didn't want Martha out of his sight. She had always been a free spirit, like a songbird with a melody in her heart, and whenever I saw her a few years later, she had withered and wilted. She ended up depressed, withdrawn, and she had Alzheimer's. She wound up in a memory care facility in Memphis. I believe her way out was to give up."

"Ugh, that really is so sad. And scary."

"I realized the risk was too high. I would not lose my happiness and free spirit for the sake of having another husband. I refuse to be trapped in a cruel relationship and too old to get out."

"That makes a lot of sense," I say. I think of my mom, happy alone in her big old house on the hill, the house she raised us in. She lives in the woods. She has Ring security cameras on every door. Whenever there is movement in front of the camera, she gets an alert on her phone. The alert sounds like wind chimes. Sometimes it's triggered by a branch flopping dramatically in the wind. It is sometimes the Amazon delivery guy. But the cameras make her feel safe in her house in the forest.

We drive in silence for a bit. The Dandy story has Mom looking out the window. "But you know," she says, sitting up straight, looking down the road ahead, "love happens. If he shows up, that would be nice."

She gives a flat-mouthed smile to the window. Allowing a little moment of wondering.

I picture "him" and wonder what he would be like. James Brolin in a Cadillac. A deacon in the church. He'd tell my mother that she's beautiful every day.

I wonder if she really longs for him, or allows herself to do so. Maybe I am in my partnering years and just projecting on her what she doesn't even really want. She's been married. Twice. And both men broke her heart. The romance of love has, for her, been a farce. But is it dead? Maybe she's perfectly happy. Or maybe she's not allowing herself to long for him, for hope is poison.

I wonder if my husband is out there. If he is my first husband, or my only husband, or maybe we don't even use the typical spousal language. Maybe he's just my guy. *What you seek is also seeking you,* the internet tells me Rumi says. I love that thought. Is my husband at a coffee shop right now, completely unaware of me as I am of him? Is my mom's future man reading a book right now, on a porch, wondering if he'll ever love again?

I once again try putting on the news. Just the NPR hourly newscast. Just a quick bite. It's only four minutes of NPR, I think. Mom will be fine.

But Lakshmi Singh is telling us of Covid death numbers, vaccine efficacy, the updates we've become accustomed to. She says that the FDA is investigating the heightened number of thrombosis blood clots in those who got the Johnson & Johnson shot.

"You know that's what gave Meme a stroke," Mom says. "A blood clot from surgery."

"I think I knew that. I thought it was just a stroke. It was from surgery?"

"Meme needed her spleen out and she was very scared of doctors and didn't want to do it. And I wish she'd come to Nashville where the doctors are good. But her and Papa decided they wanted to do it in Poplar Bluff. She went in for the surgery and had massive strokes on both sides of her brain during and after surgery and was never the same again."

"Wow, I didn't know that. I'm so sorry, Mom."

"So, you know, I have real reasons to be hesitant."

"I see that," I say, suddenly rewriting my assumptions. I pull up the file "Mom is unvaccinated because she is brainwashed by conservative talk radio" and add a new memo to it: "Mom worries about blood clots and strokes because her mother died from one after surgery."

"That's why I try to take good care of myself. Colloidal silver. Vitamins. Gardening. And swimming at the gym."

"And you've made me want to take care of myself too."

"We've got good genes," she says, "but we also gotta do what we can."

"I took the vaccines because I trust experts, the epidemiologists. I know in your circles and news and stuff it's all about thinking for yourself and distrusting the elites, but I just don't buy it. I don't think that there's some cabal of liars trying to trick us, to put poison in us to control us. Humans don't work together like that."

"I think they do," she says.

Ugh. I'm not arguing. I turn down NPR until I can find something else to listen to. I want my brain to relax. What can I play? I got it. I go to Spotify and find a playlist called "Hits of the '70s." The decade when my mom was in her twenties. I hit Shuffle, and "It's Too Late" by Carole King comes on.

"Oh," she tilts her head like a puppy. "I love this song."

This will buy us a few hundred happy miles.

The rest of the trip melts away. We are horses headed back to the stable. No sights to see. Only miles to cover. We drive long days, energized by the thought of home.

Wyoming gives way to Nebraska, then Missouri, then southern Illinois. When we stop for food, I check Zillow. How much are farms here? Fifty acres and a farmhouse and a barn for $375K. I could make a life here. "Writer lives in the country, shuns society." The landscape gently lifts from plains to rolling hills. It begins to look like Tennessee. Like home.

A specific image keeps churning in my mind. My mom cresting the sand dune in Florence, looking at the Pacific. Her eyes were young, her face a timeless balance of youth and a life lived, history and wonder. I saw discovery *and* remembrance in her face.

I can't stop seeing it. And I know it is how I will remember her forever.

We cross into Tennessee and most of the leaves are gone from the trees. The sky is crisp blue. The trees are gray with just a few stubborn leaves here and there. We pull into Nashville around midafternoon, just two and a half days after leaving the Pacific Ocean. We've passed over mountains and plains and more mountains and farms and back to the tree-covered hills of home. As any traveler knows, the return is rarely accompanied by a sense of closure. The bigness of the trip whimpers into the driveway. Plopping my bag in my room. Dreading the unpack. Opening the fridge to see what's in it, not looking for anything specific. We're back where we began. And was it even real?

My mission was twofold: to get to know more about my mom, and to ask her that big looming question. I did both. I love her more by knowing her more. I also didn't get the answer I wanted. Maybe I expected the answer that I got. But in my littlest secret hope, the hope I feared to face, I wished for the other one.

But I am home now. And I have no hope. I have the truth. And love for my mother. And she loves me.

We take our bags to our rooms. We unpack.

"I'll get the fire going and we can watch something," Mom says. "There are lots of sparkling waters in the fridge." And we drop back into our routine.

9

. . .

Last April, I hosted a writing retreat in Boone, North Carolina. I've never done such a thing, and I wouldn't have done it if the venue hadn't reached out and asked me to, or if I hadn't needed the money. Hosting a writer's retreat triggered a specific fear: imposter's syndrome. To teach writing, you have to *really* be a writer. You have to know exactly why you make the decisions you do. Why you word things one way and not another. These are things I haven't studied and don't know. My only teacher has been reading. Soaking myself in language for thirty years. I write until it sounds right. Until how it is on the page is how I would say it out loud. When the retreat center asked if I'd ever consider hosting, I felt like the universe was inviting me into discomfort, into something new.

I said yes and we did it on a cold April weekend high in the

Blue Ridge Mountains. One hundred fifteen people came, and I led them in writing exercises, reading in front of the crowd, watching short films, and playing camp games. I built the weekend as I would want to experience it. One part documentary film festival, one part writing assignments, one part long hikes, one part charades in an open field. It went well. Almost everyone who came had read my books and was already buttered up to enjoy it. They were mostly just excited to spend the weekend with an author they liked. This made the audience very forgiving and activated. No one sat in the back with their arms crossed.

On the second day I asked them to walk in the woods silently for forty-five minutes, saying nothing, and then sit under a tree and write for forty-five minutes. I told them to write things they'd never written down, things they'd never allowed themselves to think. Things that would get them in trouble. Things that felt nasty or mean or scary or vulnerable. "Write it down," I said, "and then we'll burn it in a bonfire tonight." I wanted them to feel how powerful it is to put language to secret thoughts. When you write down your shame, your failures, your dark or embarrassing deeds, they no longer lurk like a monster behind the door. They come into view and are left weaker for it. Often, they are no monster, just a jacket on the coat rack.

As we gathered around the fire, I expected people to start throwing in their pages without fanfare. They were secrets, after all. I just felt that the act of burning would give the writing a gravitas. And it's hard to get 115 people to be quiet, especially outdoors around a fire sized for ten people. But something started happening. An energy took over the crowd. Someone said, "I'll start," as if we were waiting, and I guess we were. She said, "I wrote that I am tired of being depressed and feeling like no one can understand me. Meeting you all, being here, reminds me that I'm not alone, so fuck that shit." Then she threw her paper in the fire.

The group clapped and laughed with delighted support. Then, as if it had been planned all along, one by one people started telling the group what they wrote. "I wrote that I am lonely in my marriage and I think my husband married an idea of me, not the real me. I'm miserable." "I don't know what I'm good at and I'm worried that I'm not good at anything, and I want to burn that lie." "I've had body issues my whole life, I can't imagine anyone touching me, and I don't want to hold on to that anymore." Some cried. Others didn't. Most voices shook. A few were steady and pushed out their confessions with strong will. More and more people spoke. "OK, fine, I wasn't going to share, but I wrote that I am a writer, and I've denied myself that I am one, and I have to own that and get rid of the fear."

I hadn't planned to share, as I hadn't written anything. Well, I did do the silent walk and I did write in my journal, but I didn't write burning secrets. I wrote what it was like to disconnect and sit by a stream. But the spirit of something had taken over this fire circle. The air was full of energy. One girl said, "I think we should sing!" and a few people laughed. But after a couple more shares, she started singing. "Take me hooome, country road . . ." Then we all came in, "to the place, we belong!" And the voices rose in unison. Most people in the circle had been raised in a church—evangelical, Mormon, Catholic, or some other version of faith. The thought came to me, *Wow, we are religious creatures. We get together, we feel the "spirit" and we want to sync up in ecstatic experience.* We sang the chorus two times through and felt closer for it. A unit. An army of tender loves. We stopped and laughed in some mysterious recognition.

After something like forty people had spoken, I felt the lateness of the hour and decided to get up and talk. *I'm the host of the retreat,* I thought. *I probably should.* I fished in my pocket and found a crumpled receipt. I folded it to look like a piece of paper I'd written on, and held it in my hand as I stood up. What could I say that was on par with the intensity and vulnerability of this group? How could I honor the spirit of this moment?

I tried to search my body for an answer. *What do I fear to write?* And what kept coming up was the very subject of this book. I want my mom to approve of me. I want to receive her blessing. I don't want to talk about that, which means I should talk about it. I started talking.

"OK so the book I'm writing right now is about how we want the approval of our parents, and sometimes we don't get it, and we fight for it, and how scary it is to ask for it. In 2020, I had the most surprising conversation with my dad. He, without warning, said, 'You know, Jed, when you get married, to a man I mean, whenever that is, I'd be happy to walk you down the aisle.'"

Right as I began to quote my dad in front of everyone, I started crying. The kind of crying where your throat closes and words won't come out, because if you push, they squeak. The insult of getting emotional: you sound like a dog toy.

Everyone around the fire was listening with such love, their eyes so caring. There is a special alchemy in moments like this. Confession in front of a loving group. The feeling of support. Of opened hearts. For some reason, saying that my dad had given me this approval flooded me. I pushed and pushed to finish the story. And after long whimpering pauses, I got it out.

"It was a permission, and approval, I never even expected, I never dared ask for. I had built my adulthood separate from all that. And somehow he gave it to me, completely as a surprise. And it really meant a lot to me. But the truth is, the real approval I wanted was from my mother. And we went on this big road trip, and I knew the whole time I had to be brave and ask her, because it was my final fear, the final boss in the video game of my life. And so I asked her, 'When I get gay married, will you come to the wedding?' and she said, 'No. I can't.'"

The crowd let out a gasp. Clutching their hearts. Eyebrows furrowed with compassion. They knew my mom from my stories, from my posts on Instagram, from the way I talk about her and travel with her. They love her. Everyone does. And this was not what they expected me to say.

"And so, my final boss was the fear of her rejecting me. Of her saying no. But she said it. And you know what? She still loves me, and I love her too. And it's . . . freer now. My love for her is not conditional on her approving every part of me. And now I don't have to wonder. I have my answer. And I guess what I had to learn was that I can't wait for permission to live. The only approval I need is the approval of my own heart. My own soul. And when she said no, it sort of set me free. That I'm not waiting anymore. I'm free."

I tossed the receipt into the fire and everyone said "yes" and "amen" and did those slow deliberate claps of affirmation. I felt good for sharing and good for crying. Something released. I felt nourished. Strong and safe. I thanked everyone for their vulnerability and tenderness and support for each other, and we lingered around the fire in conversation. People came up to hug me. My friend Orion said, "In the twelve years I've known you, I've never seen you cry like that."

"I don't know what came over me!" I said.

I was high on the endorphins and adrenaline of communal emotion. The ecstasy of vulnerability in front of a safe army of helpers.

Then one of the attendees, Rebekah, came up to me with a face full of something to say.

She hugged me hard. "I know we've just met but I really do love you."

"I feel the love—"

"But listen to me." She took me by the shoulders. "Here's how I see it. There is no final boss. This conversation with your mom isn't the final boss. Life doesn't work that way. The bosses keep coming. One fight survived leads to the next one that you couldn't have imagined. You finally feel safe to love whomever you want, and then you find there are new bosses in loving another person, building a life with someone. New, terrible bosses. Then having kids. New bosses. The true final boss is knowing that it's beyond the bosses, it's the knowledge that with every fight, you survive. You thought that was the end, and you made it through. You are stronger than you think. You survive."

I hugged her hard and thanked her for her words.

I think of the bosses in my mom's life. Overcoming her poor, dirt-floor childhood. A brutal mother who belittled her. Finding the love of her life and fame and then watching it crash and die. Finding love again and losing another husband to infidelity. Kids with health problems, addiction, and a sexuality that she was taught to fear. Money drying up. Losing her Colorado land. And now the son she spilled blood to raise writes books about her, where she is the source of conflict. The bosses keep coming.

As Rebekah walked away, I felt drained from a daylong exchange with 115 people. I was damp with exhaustion.

I started to sneak out of the fire circle and to my room, but I was in the middle of the blob of people. As I made my way to the outskirts, a few girls caught me. One of them said, "I have such a hard time with my mom. We basically have no relationship. I know she loves me, but it's so hard to be around her. How do you do it? How do you stay close and not let it hurt you?"

I dug into my last gasps of energy and ventured a response. "I can't speak for anyone else, but I moved away to California and built a life for myself. Not all of this was conscious, but I know that something in my heart knew that I might lose my whole family, I'd come out as gay and lose absolutely everyone. So as a fail-safe, I moved across the country to build my own thing, just in case that happened. I think that gave me some feeling of safety, the ability to establish real boundaries. These things are incredibly hard, but I have a choice to make—do I want my mother in my life, or don't I? And I choose that I do."

Another girl chimed in, "Well, you can be friends with your mom because she has redeeming qualities. Mine doesn't. My mom and my dad abused me my whole life, really traumatically, and they don't like me and they abused me, my uncles too. I never felt safe. I still don't as an adult. It's a big deal that she loves you, and you feel that."

Like a splash of cold water, I was embarrassed at my life. At all I had said and cried over. Yes, evangelical Christianity left me with a delayed knowledge of body and intimacy, a web of shame that no one deserves. Yes, I mourn that I have a worldview rift with my mother. But my God, it could've been different.

I told her how sorry I was. I spoke what I had left in me. I told her that some boundaries are clear. And when someone molests you, harms you, is unrepentant and cruel, then let the relationship

be severed. I hugged her for a long time. I felt stupid for even of-
fering a response, but she was asking for one with her face. She
wanted to be seen and heard. So I tried. And felt like my words
were stiff and rote. Some life is so cruel, I either freeze in response
or fill the air with words.

I went back to my room, wondering when it is time to leave
and when it's worth it to remain.

I've noticed a general sentiment of discourse online—that lack
of total acceptance is total rejection. The thought goes like this: If
your family says they love you *but* they can't accept your sexuality,
they aren't allowed to say they love you. They don't love all of you,
therefore they don't love you. You have to draw a boundary and say
"that's not acceptable" and remove them from your life.

These statements get thousands of reposts and clapping hands.
I always feel conflicted when I read them. Maybe they're exactly
right. My identity isn't up for debate. And while some parent
"wrestled" with the question of who their kid can be, the kid lost
his youth to shame and confusion. I've seen the lack of acceptance,
the church cherry-picking scripture, the threat of exile, lead to
compartmentalized minds and an unshakable fear of intimacy. I've
seen it force gay men into heterosexual marriages, only to watch
them blow up and leave young kids reeling from the fallout. I've
seen it lead people to the clergy, creating a church full of sexually
repressed men who fermented into monsters of molestation.

But I cannot excommunicate. Me, I cannot. Maybe others can.
Maybe they should. I don't know where the line between true
identity and trauma-response or faulty brain chemistry should be
drawn. But I know that who I feel myself to be is good, and not
broken. I know that all the shame of Christian teachings couldn't
shake the gnawing conviction of my desires. And when the heart

and the brain are on the same side, dogma hardly stands a chance. I also know that my mom is a good person, following the convictions of her heart and her head. I know that she doesn't feel what I feel, and she has had a lifetime of teachers telling her to distrust her own beliefs, to trust in a book before her thoughts.

I was able to build enough distance and safety in my life to see her clearly. If I hadn't left, found my own way, the claustrophobia of living under her wing would've metastasized into rage. I would've hated her. Not because she is evil, but because my anger would have been necessary to set me free. To make me demand space and run.

But I see her, and I love her, and I know she is good and beautiful. I have my space, and I am standing on my own feet.

I WANT MY MOTHER in my life. And I will fight for that. And I will let it be a middle thing. Not quite full, but not lost. A love that limps.

AFTER THE RETREAT, I drive back to Nashville and spend a few days at Mom's. Even though we've just done a big once-in-a-lifetime road trip, there is a constant hum of duty. The expectation that we have breakfast together and watch a show at night. The rest of the day can be mine. To see friends. To work out. To get some writing done and go out for dinner and drinks. But breakfast together and TV at night are a pattern we've built. And I can feel Mom hoping for them. She wants more. She wants the whole day, every day, but she would never say that. Every time is a humble offer. "Can I make you some eggs and toast this morning?" she says, coming into the sitting room where I am reading and drinking coffee. She says it as if the idea just came to her.

One night I finish dinner with my friends at nine and realize that's plenty early to get home and watch something with Mom. She usually sits in her recliner by the gas fireplace until eleven or midnight. This is her nightly routine. Get in her cozy spot by the fire, maybe a blanket over her legs, alone in her big house, and watch a movie or a show. She can really binge. Blast through an entire TV series in two days. She doesn't like sex, but she loves violence. Espionage. Crime. Family intrigue. Having burned through all of the American dramas that aren't too raunchy, she has begun traveling the world in search of more entertainment. She's watched every Colombian show available for streaming. Now she's moved to Russian dramas. Korea will certainly be next. When I scroll through her Netflix home page, it is completely unfamiliar to me. Period pieces set in Bogotá. Aliens on the pyramids.

I come home and sit in the matching recliner next to hers. They frame the fireplace and are pointed at the huge TV mounted on the wall. She is watching a show about ancient aliens. How maybe they jump-started human civilization and pushed us out of apehood.

When I sit down, she doesn't ask me about my day. She doesn't ask me about dinner. These would have been expected. "Do you believe in aliens?" she says instead. "Do you know anyone who's been abducted?"

I love a surprise.

"Actually, yes and yes. I mean, I believe they're real. I don't care if they are or aren't, but it seems like they must be. I actually have a friend who is dead serious about being abducted, he says over six hundred times when he was young. He can't say anything else about it. And he's the funnest, coolest, brightest person. He thinks they're studying his reproduction. Like they can't reproduce anymore, so they're abducting people and studying how we reproduce."

"I believe in them too," she says. "A Bible teacher I listen to, on a podcast, says that they're satanic fallen demons created by Lucifer to destroy our free will and deceive us and stop the seed of God and God's DNA."

"Oh my," I say. Now that is some Sherry Shriner shit. I guess I still have some tequila in me, or I'm tired, because I don't censor myself. "Well, I don't believe in free will, so I guess I don't believe they're sent here to destroy it."

Why did I say that? Why am I compelled to fight?

"What do you mean, you don't believe in free will?" she asks, perking up in disbelief.

"I think choice is an illusion." Here I go. Words rush out. "I don't think it makes sense. And honestly, almost every neuroscientist and person who studies the brain agrees with me. If you really think about it, what even is a choice? Every choice is a preference built out of some prior programming. If you like the taste of pizza more than sushi, that isn't a choice, you don't choose pizza, you can't help your taste buds. If you want to go on a walk versus stay in and watch TV, and you choose a walk, why? What was that choice? It was a feeling. You didn't choose to feel like you wanted to walk. You just do."

I can hear myself talking, making no sense to her intuitions. My mother looks at me like I'm a stranger in her house.

Her voice jumps into outrage. "Then we don't need churches. We don't need the gospel. We don't need to evangelize or help the poor. That doesn't make any sense!"

"That's why it's called 'the illusion of free will.' It feels like all these things matter. And even if we agree that free will doesn't matter, it'll still feel like we're making choices all the time. I believe choice is just some uncanny valley between brain function and consciousness."

"Why would Jesus need to die on the cross, then?" she says in high-pitched disbelief.

"Why do volcanoes erupt? I don't know, they just do!" I can feel the conversation shifting from sparring match to offense.

"I'm sorry, but that just sounds selfish and lazy," she says. "You need to ask God what he thinks about that."

"I've been asking God for twenty years. This is what God said to me, through science and reason."

"You're saying I didn't choose to divorce your father?"

"I mean, it feels like you did. But I don't think you chose that. Like, I don't think oil chooses not to mix with water. It just does what it was designed to do."

"I didn't choose to go on the walk with your father? I didn't choose to sell the farm? Yes I did. I could've done something else. If you don't choose, there is no right and wrong."

"Exactly."

She's shaking her head. "Well, you really need to ask God about this again. I choose to love my kids! You think I love you because I can't help it?"

"Absolutely. Can't you feel that your love for your kids is something more than choice? Like an instinct?"

"But I choose. I choose the hard things. To help the poor. To be long-suffering. To tithe. To repent. To wait upon the Lord. That is what it means to be a Christian. To choose to follow Jesus. That is the salvation of the Gospel. If you don't believe in choice, then you don't believe in the Gospel."

"But Mom, the entire Calvinist church doesn't believe in choice. That's the whole thing. Predestination. That is a major church denomination that doesn't believe in free will. I think they got it right. And they are definitely Christians."

"Well, they believe that God foreknew the choices they would make. They still make them, but God knew in advance."

"What does that even mean? If God makes a person, and God makes a person knowing the choices they will make, then God made the choices for the person!"

"If you don't believe in choice, then what is the point of being a human, having a soul??"

I stop myself before saying that I don't believe in souls. This conversation has no end. It is too foundational. You can't debate the bedrock underneath a metropolis. There's too much on top to rethink the base.

"I don't know," I finally say. "I just know that choice doesn't make sense to me. OK, I'm going to bed Momma, I love you."

Her face transforms from bewildered horror to a warm smile.

"Ooh, I just love conversations like this!" she says, clasping her hands. "I used to have conversations like this all the time when I was younger, at seminary, it's been a while and I love it!" Her tone has flipped like a switch. As if her exasperation was a performance.

I laugh in shock. "I do too," I say, shaking my head. "Sweet dreams, Mom."

"Good night, honey. I love you even though I can't choose it.

I'm programmed to love you and pray for you against my will, which doesn't exist."

"Exactly right," I say.

THE NEXT MORNING, I wake to the smell of bacon and eggs coming from the kitchen. I waddle in looking for coffee and she's swirling the eggs in the skillet. "Good morning, honey! I'm choosing to make you breakfast."

POSTSCRIPT

· · ·

AFTER OUR ROAD TRIP, I bought my mom a vintage locket necklace with an elephant on it. I put a picture of me inside. A promise
to my mom that I will believe in the whole elephant, even if I can't
see it. And an invitation to her to believe in it for me, too.

ACKNOWLEDGMENTS

• • •

Thank you Mom for being big enough to be analyzed in public. For loving attention, even if it's complex. For loving me, even if I'm complex.

Thank you Kenny Laubbacher for sparking the idea for this book, and Glenda Copeland for confirming that spark.

Thank you Derek Reed for knowing what I'm trying to say and finding it buried in the basement.

Thank you Tina Constable for seeing me before I saw myself.

Thank you Bryan Norman for plucking me out of the air.

Thank you everyone at Convergent and Penguin Random House for making me feel like a queen.

About the Author

. . .

JEDIDIAH JENKINS is a travel writer, an entrepreneur, and the author of two *New York Times* bestsellers, *To Shake the Sleeping Self* and *Like Streams to the Ocean*. A graduate of USC and Pepperdine University School of Law, Jenkins began his professional career with the nonprofit Invisible Children, where he helped orchestrate multinational campaigns to end the use of child soldiers in central Africa. His parents, Peter and Barbara Jenkins, are the authors of the bestselling A Walk Across America series. He is the executive editor of *Wilderness* magazine. Jenkins's work has appeared in *The Paris Review* and *Playboy,* and his story has been covered by *National Geographic.*

jedidiahjenkins.com
Instagram: @jedidiahjenkins

ABOUT THE TYPE

· · ·

This book was set in Caslon, a typeface first designed in 1722 by William Caslon (1692–1766). Its widespread use by most English printers in the early eighteenth century soon supplanted the Dutch typefaces that had formerly prevailed. The roman is considered a "workhorse" typeface due to its pleasant, open appearance, while the italic is exceedingly decorative.

EMERGENCY CONTACT

NAME: Jedidiah Jenkins

EMERGENCY CONTACT: Barbara Jenkins   RELATION: mother

More from
JEDIDIAH JENKINS

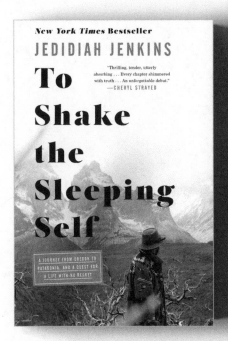

CONVERGENT

Available wherever books are sold